# Unlocking Your Potential:
# A Journey to Self-Development

**Farah W. Eida**

# Table of Contents


Introduction ..................................................................................................i

Chapter 1: Understanding Yourself.................................................................1

The Significance of Self-Awareness ...........................................2

If you lack self-awareness, what will happen? .........................3

Exploring Self-Awareness:..........................................................4

What are the Benefits of Self-Awareness? ...............................6

Improved Decision-Making: .......................................................6

It can help in making our relationships better: .......................7

Personal Growth: ........................................................................8

Ways that can help you to cultivate self-awareness: ..............9

Be mindful:...................................................................................9

Journaling Prompts:..................................................................10

Feedback and Self-Assessment: ..............................................10

Practical Exercises:...................................................................11

Chapter 2: Setting Meaningful Goals............................................................13

The Power of Goal Setting in Personal Development...................14

Why People Still Fail When They Set Goals?..............................15

What is the Impact of Having Goals?..........................................16

Direction and Clarity:...........................................................16

Motivation and Accountability: ...........................................17

Measurement of Progress:....................................................17

A Step-by-Step Guide to Setting Realistic and Inspiring Goals ..... 18

Step 1: Self-Reflection ................................................................. 18

Step 2: SMART Goals Framework........................................... 19

Step 3: Break Down Goals ......................................................20

Step 4: Prioritization and Focus ...........................................21

Step 5: Visualize and Affirm..................................................22

Step 6: Regular Review and Adaptation...............................22

Chapter 3: Overcoming Challenges ............................................24

Common Obstacles in Personal Growth...................................25

Some of the Common Challenges: ...........................................25

Self-Doubt and Fear: ..............................................................25

Procrastination and Lack of Discipline:................................26

External Pressures and Criticism: .........................................27

Strategies for Overcoming Setbacks and Building Resilience ......29

Cultivating a Growth Mindset:...............................................29

Self-Compassion and Acceptance: .........................................30

Goal Reevaluation and Adaptation: .......................................31

Developing Resilience through Adversity:..............................32

Mindfulness and Stress Management: .....................................33

Learn from Setbacks:...............................................................34

Persistence and Consistency: ..................................................35

Chapter 4: Building Positive Habits............................................36

The Role of Habits in Shaping Our Lives ................................37

Understanding Habit Formation:..............................................38

Impact of Habits: ...................................................................39

    Routine and Efficiency:...............................................39

    Behaviour Reinforcement: .........................................40

Practical Advice on Developing and Maintaining Positive Habits 41

    Identify Keystone Habits:...........................................41

    Start Small and Specific: ............................................42

    Consistency and Repetition:........................................43

    Trigger and Routine:...................................................44

    Accountability and Tracking:......................................45

    Focus on Behaviour, Not Outcome: ...........................46

    Embrace Slip-ups with Compassion:..........................46

Chapter 5 Mindfulness and Emotional Intelligence ......................48

Mindfulness:...................................................................49

How mindfulness can help you: .....................................50

    Reduced Stress:...........................................................50

    Improved Mental Clarity:............................................50

    Enhanced Emotional Regulation: ...............................51

    The connection between mindfulness and emotional intelligence: 52

    Emotional Intelligence: ..............................................52

    Improved Relationships: .............................................54

    Enhanced Self-Awareness:..........................................55

    Effective Conflict Resolution:.....................................56

Exercises to Enhance Self-Awareness and Empathy ......57

    Mindful Breathing Exercise: ......................................57

    Body Scan Meditation:................................................57

Emotional Journaling: ...................................................................57

Active Listening Practice: ...........................................................58

Perspective-Taking Exercise: .....................................................59

Meditation: ...................................................................................59

Chapter 6: Cultivating Gratitude ..............................................60

Benefits of Gratitude: ..................................................................61

Mental Health Boost: ...................................................................61

Enhanced Relationships: ..............................................................62

Physical Health Benefits: .............................................................63

Exercises for Cultivating Gratitude in Daily Life.........................64

Chapter 7: Effective Communication..........................................68

Ask yourself, "ARE YOU A GOOD COMMUNICATOR?".......69

The Importance of Clear and Empathetic Communication ...........69

Benefits of Effective Communication: .........................................70

Building Trust:...............................................................................70

Conflict Resolution:......................................................................71

Strengthening Relationships:........................................................72

Tips for Improving Interpersonal Relationships...........................73

1. Active Listening: ......................................................................73

2. Clarity and Conciseness: ..........................................................73

3. Empathy and Understanding:....................................................74

4. Open and Honest Communication:............................................76

5. Conflict Resolution Skills: .......................................................77

6. Feedback and Validation:..........................................................78

Chapter 8: Financial Well-being ........................................................ 80

Relationship between Financial Health and Personal Development: 81

Freedom and Opportunities:................................................ 81

Reduced Stress:.................................................................. 82

Long-Term Planning: ......................................................... 83

Guidance on Budgeting, Saving, and Investing Wisely ............... 84

1. Budgeting:..................................................................... 84

2. Emergency Fund and Savings:......................................... 85

3. Debt Management: .......................................................... 86

4. Retirement Planning:....................................................... 86

5. Financial Education and Learning: ................................... 87

6. Mindful Spending and Value Assessment:........................ 88

Chapter 9: Nurturing Relationships........................................................ 89

Impact of Relationships on Personal Fulfilment: ......................... 90

Emotional Support and Understanding:................................ 90

Growth and Learning: ........................................................ 91

Fulfillment and Happiness: ................................................. 92

Insights on Fostering Healthy Connections................................. 93

1. Communication and Empathy: ......................................... 94

2. Mutual Respect and Boundaries: ..................................... 95

3. Quality Time and Presence: ............................................ 95

4. Support and Encouragement:........................................... 96

5. Conflict Resolution and Forgiveness:............................... 97

6: Cultivate Trust and Reliability:........................................ 98

7. Gratitude and Appreciation: ...................................................... 99

Chapter 10: Continuous Learning ................................................ 100

The Value of Lifelong Learning ................................................. 101

Importance of Lifelong Learning: .............................................. 103

Adaptation to Change: .......................................................... 103

Personal Growth and Fulfillment: .............................................. 104

Skill Enhancement and Innovation: ............................................. 104

Resources and Strategies for Ongoing Personal Development ... 105

1. Reading and Self-Education: ................................................. 105

2. Networking and Communities: ................................................ 106

3. Mentorship and Coaching: ................................................... 107

4. Skill Development and Practice: ............................................ 108

5. Podcasts and Audiobooks: ................................................... 109

6. Reflection and Application: ................................................ 109

Conclusion: .................................................................... 111

# Introduction

"Unlocking Your Potential: A Journey to Self-Development" aims to be a guiding light on the path to personal growth and fulfilment. This book is designed to empower readers with insightful guidance and actionable strategies to uncover their true potential. By exploring various facets of self-awareness, goal setting, resilience, mindfulness, and more, it offers a comprehensive roadmap for individuals seeking to embark on a transformative journey toward a more enriched and purposeful life.

I remember the time when I felt stuck in a cycle of uncertainty and dissatisfaction. It was a pivotal moment when I realized that despite external achievements, something within me was yearning for growth and fulfilment. I embarked on a journey of self-reflection and exploration, motivational posts/articles, engaging in reflective practices, and seeking guidance from mentors.

One insight that sparked my transformation was the realization that my mindset and habits played a profound role in shaping my experiences. I discovered the power of cultivating a positive mindset and how intentional habits could propel me toward my goals. It was a gradual but empowering process, where small changes in my daily routine led to significant shifts in my perspective and life trajectory.

This personal journey ignited my passion for self-development. It inspired me to share the transformative tools and principles I learned along the way, motivating others to embark on their paths toward unlocking their potential.

# Chapter 1:
# Understanding Yourself

*"One's self is well hidden from one's self; of all mines of treasure, one's own is the last to be dug up."*
*—Friedrich Nietzsche*

I noticed that when I felt stuck in a cycle of uncertainty and dissatisfaction, I tried to improve myself by doing things my way. I was making a lot of effort to modify it. It took me some time to realize that if I wanted to alter the path of my life, I needed to be aware of certain realities. The first of these was gaining the knowledge necessary to change the trajectory of my life.

## The Significance of Self-Awareness

The first thing to understand is that self-awareness is not like a sudden flash of enlightenment or a switch that somebody can easily turn on or off. It plays a major role in your self-development. There are moments when we are more self-aware of our lives than at other times, and our level of self-awareness varies. Self-awareness can be defined as a conscious perception of our thoughts, feelings, events, and behaviours, both internal and external, that is firmly grounded. This perception can be either internal or external.

When our actions are motivated by unconscious urges and biases, we are unable to perceive patterns in the environment around us. As a result, we are unable to take any proactive measures to alter our circumstances. If we do not have a solid foundation of self-awareness, it is impossible to possess a great number of other positive characteristics and attributes. However, there is very little information available that teaches us how to develop this foundation inside ourselves. And why would we, considering that most of us believe that we already possess self-awareness? Foremost, you must know what self-awareness is. The concept of self-awareness refers to the ability to recognize the difference between who you believe you are and *who you actually are*. It also involves comprehending the difference between the person you aspire to be and the person you are.

## If you lack self-awareness, what will happen?

I can still vividly recollect the moments when I was so unaware of myself. It was as if I were living each day completely blind to my shortcomings as well as the repercussions that my actions had on those around me.

If you do not have self-awareness, it will not only affect your own life, but it will also affect the lives of other people. This is something that you need to learn. Acquire the knowledge that if you are not impacting others, do not allow others to affect you as well. Avoid creating obstacles for other people and allowing them to impede your life.

It is difficult to trust your judgment and recognize whether your mental or physical health is stable if you lack self-awareness. The likelihood of experiencing life on your own terms decreases if you do not have a firm grasp on your innermost thoughts and feelings. Instead, you will be so influenced by other people's opinions that you will live your life according to their ideas of what you *"should"* be.

Feelings of inadequacy, anger, anxiety, resentment, and hollowness may persist when your life is not truly of your own. Sometimes, we try to force ourselves into relationships or situations that are not healthy, and we even question if our expectations are too high when they are too low. Our first plan for our lives never materializes because we either lack confidence in our abilities or knowledge of what it would entail, and as a result, we settle for less-than-ideal alternatives. It is an issue, and it is quite probable that low self-esteem and lack of self-awareness are foundational causes that can hinder your self-development.

## Exploring Self-Awareness:

Becoming self-aware is coming to terms with the fact that, although you can completely indulge in your fantasies and fulfil your deepest desires, you cannot have everything that you require. It is hard but not impossible to have, be, or accomplish everything. The ability to make a bunch of people laugh like Kevin Hart or create innovations that change the world like Steve Jobs are all very difficult feats. Because each of us possesses a unique set of skills, capabilities, inclinations, and blessings that make us more suitable for some professional fields than others, we all have a unique set of abilities.

As you develop self-awareness, you will begin to notice changes in your thoughts and perspectives. An important component in achieving this mental shift is an increase in your self-knowledge and a shift in your emotions. So, the main question is, how can you explore yourself?

The first step in developing self-awareness is to become curious about your true thoughts and feelings. This is easier said than done, however, as it is easy to numb yourself to unpleasant emotions and thoughts in order to maintain a smooth life. It could be challenging to make the connection between your physical and emotional well-being if you have developed a habit of convincing yourself that things are not that bad at work, which might lead to diminishing your discomfort. Some good places to start when trying to connect with your inner self are by writing down your thoughts and feelings or even just talking about how you are feeling. Your inner critic is likely to start speaking up as you work on this. Becoming curious about its meaning can be beneficial when this occurs. Your inner critic usually emerges when you are scared or when you are trying to silence a critical voice from your past. Attempting to maintain objectivity as you explore your conflicting feelings is one approach to listening to this voice.

When talking about myself, I often found myself being overly critical. It took me some time to realize that the inner critic I was hearing was actually my own voice. I realized that the one being hard on myself was none other than me. I am conscious of the fact that this is true not just for me, but also for others. Changing this viewpoint is crucial. Without passing judgment on yourself, accept the life that awaits you. Without passing judgment on others, you will begin to transform your own life.

When I talked about myself, I was critical. It took me time to realize that my inner critic was actually me.

Simply, you will start to wonder about your interior world. When you feel negative emotions like frustration, sadness, or anger, it is best just to accept your thoughts and feelings as they come up rather than try to change them, rationalize them, or push them away. It might be challenging to identify areas that require additional study or examination when we are intimately connected to our thoughts and feelings.

One effective strategy for piercing through that mental veil is to ask yourself self-awareness questions. For instance, ask yourself if you are completely present in this instant or if you are worrying about the future or regretting the past. Do I realize how my activities may affect people around me, either favourably or unfavourably? What are my guiding principles? Have I asked for input from others to learn more about how they see me and how I affect them? In this manner, you can follow a more structured set of questions that cover a wide range of life topics. Since your answers will evolve in response to changes in perspective and life events, I recommend revisiting these questions at least a few times a year. Asking people in your inner circle, like family, friends, or a significant other; can be a terrific way to break the ice and learn more about them. In turn, you will learn more about yourself and discover aspects of them that you might not have known before.

## What are the Benefits of Self-Awareness?

Understanding the value of self-improvement can bring a range of benefits. These include boosting self-esteem, making sound decisions, fostering creativity, exercising self-control, and mastering emotional regulation. Moreover, it enhances learning and adaptability, promotes humility and self-awareness, and encourages a healthy sense of pride. Additionally, it nurtures empathy, facilitates effective communication, and strengthens cooperative abilities. One of the major benefits that it provides you is to enhance your ability to communicate and work together.

These things, on the other hand, are a result of the fact that you are self-aware of where you are and the course that your life is taking. The foundation of your journey toward personal development is the cultivation of self-awareness. Possessing an understanding of yourself is analogous to having a compass that directs you through the winding roads of life. For a deeper understanding of your actual nature, it is necessary to peel back the layers of your thoughts, feelings, and behaviours.

## Improved Decision-Making:

Understanding our values and motivations allows for more aligned and effective decisions. Effective decision-making relies on self-awareness, which impacts many parts of your thought processes and habits of behaviour. You can improve your results through better decision-making when you have a firm grasp of who you are. Several important factors allow us to delve deeper into the complex relationship between self-awareness and decision-making. To begin, being self-aware will enable you to identify your prejudices, beliefs, and values. It is common for people to bring their own biases and viewpoints into decision-making subconsciously. Being self-aware will allow you to see your own biases and determine if you are impacting your decision-making. Furthermore, decision-making relies heavily on emotional intelligence, which can be developed through self-awareness. Having emotional intelligence means being able to identify, label, and control your own emotions as well as those of other people.

## It can help in making our relationships better:

Self-awareness fosters empathy and understanding, enriching our interactions with others. Our self-awareness can help us in our relationships. A strong foundation for building better, more fulfiling relationships is self-awareness. Interactions with others can be more fruitful and satisfying when people have a firm grasp on their own feelings, communication preferences, and basic needs. Empathy, communication, conflict resolution, and relationship satisfaction are some of how self-awareness affects relationships. Being empathetic is a crucial part of being self-aware in relationships. Being empathetic means you can put yourself in another person's shoes and experience what they are feeling. Being in tune with one's own emotions makes one more sensitive to the feelings of those around them, which in turn makes one more empathetic. When people are more attuned to the feelings and experiences of those around them, they are better able to meet those needs and build stronger bonds with those they are intimately involved with.

## Personal Growth:

It catalyzes growth, enabling us to identify patterns and evolve positively. One's capacity for self-awareness is a potent catalyst for development. Each person can set out on a path of meaningful personal growth when they have a firm grasp of their own unique set of skills, values, emotions, and social dynamics. On this path, we must establish significant objectives, adjust to setbacks, strengthen our resilience, and forge important connections with others. As a driving force behind constructive transformation and progress, self-awareness is an essential component of maturation. People are better able to face life's obstacles, make educated decisions, and progress when they have a thorough knowledge of themselves, which includes recognizing their strengths, shortcomings, values, and goals. Being self-aware is being honest with yourself about your abilities and where you may use improvement. The first step in making deliberate attempts to better oneself is taking stock of one's strengths and weaknesses. People can become more competent and effective in general by playing to their strengths and working to improve their deficiencies. Your objectives can be advanced with its assistance. Essential components of personal growth include understanding personal values and developing meaningful goals. Individuals can better define their values and purpose in life when they have a firm grasp of their self-awareness. A sense of direction and purpose is given by this alignment, which motivates one to work toward personal improvement throughout time.

In contrast, self-aware people are often more receptive to new information and are interested in bettering themselves. This way of thinking encourages a never-ending thirst for information. Adopt yourself with a mindset of continuous learning is crucial for long-term self-improvement.

## Ways that can help you to cultivate self-awareness:

One of the most important qualities for your development is self-awareness. You must be flexible enough to adapt to the changing needs of yourself and the world around you. When you are preoccupied with pressing matters, this can become overwhelming. Are you capable of assessing the situation and swiftly altering your behaviour?

In any case, you will need to hone your self-awareness and management skills if you want to survive the challenges. This comes naturally to some people, but for others, it is a skill they have to cultivate. It is a piece of good news that self-awareness is a talent that can be developed through effort, just like any other aptitude for authority. To help you cultivate yourself for your development, here are a few things you can try:

## Be mindful:

Mindfulness is the practice of being present and aware of your thoughts and feelings without judgment, and it is a powerful tool for self-discovery. Techniques like meditation, deep breathing exercises, or mindful journaling aid in developing a heightened sense of self-awareness. The practice of mindfulness is a foundational step toward creating the life you desire. It helps you zero in on your passions and emotions, as well as your identity and how it impacts your day-to-day experiences. You can recognize the direction that your thoughts and emotions are taking you and implement any necessary changes. If you are aware of your thoughts, words, emotions, and actions, you can probably change your future. To be self-aware is to have a clear understanding of one's own identity, including one's strengths and weaknesses, thoughts and convictions, emotions, and sources of motivation. Being aware makes it easier to comprehend other people and, by extension, to discern their perceptions of you. Even if most people think they are very mindful, it is always helpful to compare yourself to others and see where you stand on a relative scale. It is possible to alter one's behaviour and convictions by remaining vigilant.

## Journaling Prompts:

People are encouraged to explore their deepest emotions and thoughts by using journal prompts. They make one think deeply about many things, including their views, values, and aspirations. Prompts allow for a deeper examination of one's inner landscape by encouraging folks to put their thoughts on paper. It is useful for seeing trends and patterns in their feelings, actions, and ideas as well. Journaling prompts can assist individuals in identifying patterns, habits, and reactions by pointing out recurrent ideas and events. If you want to know yourself better, you need to learn to recognize patterns. Positive or bad, they aid people in expressing and understanding their emotions. By letting one's feelings out, one might gain insight into their emotional reactions and evaluate events more dispassionately. Just writing down thoughts and feelings in a diary can have therapeutic effects, such as releasing pent-up tension. Some people find that writing out their feelings and thoughts helps them release those pent-up emotions. Learning to recognize and manage one's emotional reactions and coping techniques can help people become more self-aware. Keeping a journal allows us to record thoughts, feelings, and experiences. Prompts such as "What am I grateful for today?" or "What triggered certain emotions?" help delve deeper into our inner workings.

## Feedback and Self-Assessment:

Seek feedback from trusted people, and sources and engage in self-assessment exercises to provide external perspectives that complement our self-reflection. Individuals gain invaluable insights into their strengths, shortcomings, and improvement areas through feedback and self-assessment, which are essential parts of the self-awareness journey. Both methods help one grow professionally and personally by illuminating one's strengths, weaknesses, opportunities, and threats. Getting other people's opinions on your activities and behaviours is a great way to get perspective. The opinions of those around you, who may have noticed details about your character or performance that we have missed, can provide valuable perspective. To gain a better understanding of who you are, it is important to step back and look at things from the outside. It will help you to see where you can improve. Try to view constructive criticism as an asset. Constructive criticism and observations offer valuable insights.

To better understand your abilities and areas for improvement, try using both feedback and self-evaluation tools. You will be able to learn a lot about your strengths and places for growth from the constructive criticism of others. On the other hand, you can also achieve a more nuanced and balanced understanding of your strengths, and you can achieve opportunities for improvement can be achieved through self-assessment, which also stimulates reflection on one's performance and potential.

## Practical Exercises:

Test out several exercises, such as the Johari Window as a psychological model. A healthy dose of seclusion is normal, but too much secrecy can stifle open dialogue and mutual understanding in partnerships. One way to strengthen bonds and establish trust is to reveal previously unsaid details. Following that, there are parts of the unknown that neither you nor anybody else knows about that make up this aspect. Hidden talents, untapped potential, or aspects of oneself yet to be fully recognized are represented by this. Within the unknown quadrant, individuals can uncover their dormant abilities and facets of themselves previously unexplored, facilitated by self-discovery and personal growth programs. Lastly, we encounter a Blind Spot.

Blind spots are those aspects of oneself visible to others but elusive to self-awareness, encompassing habits, behaviours, or traits unnoticed by the individual A crucial strategy to reduce these blind spots involves soliciting and contemplating feedback from others, shedding light on potentially overlooked facets of oneself. Next, we have the hidden and unknown options. As individuals introspect, seek external perspectives, and become more transparent, this conceptual model evolves. The goal remains to minimize the Blind Spots, Hidden, and Unknown areas while amplifying the Open facets.

Conversely, improving oneself entails exploring one's identity through self-discovery. Resources that provide insights into your strengths, limitations, and innate tendencies include the Myers-Briggs Type Indicator (MBTI). It is critical to understand that developing self-awareness is a process rather than a destination. This chapter's strategies act as spotlights that point you in the direction of more in-depth reflection. You begin a life-changing journey to discovering your true self by honing these introspective techniques and encouraging self-reflection.

# Chapter 2:
# Setting Meaningful Goals

*"You are never too old to set another goal or to dream a new dream." — Les Brown*

# The Power of Goal Setting in Personal Development

After becoming self-aware, you need to understand the significance of goal setting in your life for your development. There is a difference between having objectives and having the correct kind of goals, yes. Most of the time, we fall into traps because we do not know how to make the proper goals for our lives, and we learn how to set goals with time.

I know you are probably asking what I mean when I say "the right kind of goals" by this point. Well, when you figure out how to make reasonable plans and goals and stick to them. Ultimately, setting goals can free you from a significant amount of life's hardships. While the concept of setting goals may seem simple, it is essential to approach it with precision and clarity. Drawing inspiration from the wisdom of countless wise individuals who have walked this path before us, the key to achieving what you truly desire in life lies in clearly defining your aspirations. Your chances of success will increase in proportion to your ability to concentrate and focus seeing any tangible results. People face their greatest challenge when they allow themselves to become distracted and stop striving for personal growth, self-development, and the achievement of their goals. People nowadays are experiencing information overload despite the ease with which anyone can access information. So first, you must know how your personal growth and self-development can depend on your goal and the life you are choosing for yourself. Goals can serve as a roadmap to your aspirations, guiding you toward your desired destinations. Setting meaningful goals is more than just an activity; it is a powerful catalyst that ignites progress and drives you closer to becoming your best self.

## Why People Still Fail When They Set Goals?

Setting standards, time, and pace for yourself is the finest aspect of goal setting. Put in more time and effort if you want to see rapid results. In life, we all aspire to accomplish our aspirations and objectives. Being a failure is something no one wants to experience. Having the ability to create goals is beneficial, but one needs to be aware of the reasons behind their failure to achieve those goals. Amazing aspirations are set by many, but few ever come to fruition. There must be some explanations, and we have to find out what they are so that we can assist you. You can figure out how to prevent them or fix them if you encounter them this way. So, are you the type of person who makes plans but never follows through?

Recognize this for what it is: a fact. Setbacks occur for millions upon billions of people every year. It is a common occurrence in anyone's life. However, we must reflect on those errors and move forward accordingly. Discovering the reasons and how to take better actions is necessary if you are like most individuals who enjoy setting goals but fail to achieve them despite all efforts.

There must have been a moment when you used to set lofty goals, and then you must have been working for some time, and then you could not accomplish those objectives. Therefore, occasionally, we do not succeed in accomplishing what we set out to do. To transform into a different kind of person, however, you will need to undergo a total transformation of who you are. You could say that if you keep this mindset, you will have a better chance of attaining your objectives and targets over time.

# What is the Impact of Having Goals?

Setting objectives is essential for your self-development and personal growth because it will establish a path for your self-improvement. It will offer direction and motivate you to work toward your goals. Having goals to work for will act as a map that will direct you along your path of personal development and exploration of who you are. It is possible to summarize the significance of establishing objectives for one's personal growth by focusing on a few essential components.

## Direction and Clarity:

The process of goal planning relies heavily on direction and clarity, which are essential in leading people to significant achievements. A compass that guides you through the complexity of life, bringing concentration and purpose, is what you get when you set your goals with a clear sense of direction.

To begin, having a well-defined destination and set of objectives is essential when defining goals. Achieving this requires deciding on a course of action that is in harmony with one's beliefs, hopes, and dreams for the future. By avoiding the traps of uncertainty and hesitation, you may be able to direct your efforts and resources more efficiently with this level of clarity of purpose. When you know where you are going, you can make decisions that get you closer to your goals and help your actions flow together. Goals provide a clear sense of direction, allowing us to focus our efforts and energies.

In addition, when you have well-defined objectives, it will be much easier to rank your various responsibilities and pursuits. You can figure out how to get where you are going after you have a clear idea of where you are going. Prioritizing tasks in this way can help you focus on the things that will have the most impact on reaching your goals.

Setting goals with a clear direction can also encourage you to tackle obstacles head-on.

### Motivation and Accountability:

Setting your goals will serve as a motivational beacon, keeping you accountable and dedicated to your aspirations. A person's level of motivation determines how much effort and excitement they put into developing and achieving goals. As guiding lights, goals motivate people by painting a picture of an ideal future. Setting objectives, whether they be long-term or short-term, can give you direction and motivate you to excel. Regardless of how difficult things get, what keeps people going is their level of motivation. One of the many advantages of goal setting is the accountability and motivation it fosters, which are powerful forces that will drive you to achieve your goals and grow as an individual. The act of creating and working toward objectives provides a structure that inherently fosters motivation and sets up a feeling of responsibility.

Moreover, a person's willingness to seek and accomplish their goals gives rise to accountability, which is an essential component of goal setting. Making a pact with yourself to achieve certain objectives fosters personal accountability. Having clear, measurable objectives that leave little space for doubt or justifications strengthens this commitment.

### Measurement of Progress:

Goals offer a yardstick to measure our growth and accomplishments. A crucial foundation for measuring growth and success in various parts of life is the formulation of goals, which act as a measure of progress. Along the way, it offers an organized strategy that will enable you to keep track of your progress, maintain your concentration on your goals, and make decisions based on accurate information during your journey toward personal growth. A tracking system that allows you to monitor and evaluate both your long-term and short-term objectives is preferable to you or anyone else. The measurement method might be made more straightforward by utilizing tracking tools and technologies. It is possible for you to methodically document and visualize your development through the use of a variety of tools, applications, and software solutions. Through the use of technology, tracking may be made more accurate and efficient, hence offering real-time insights into the accomplishment of goals.

## A Step-by-Step Guide to Setting Realistic and Inspiring Goals

Before we go any further and go into the betterment, let us first focus on the most important factor that is associated with goal setting. Should you be curious about the reasons why it is essential to make goals for your life? These are some of the steps that might assist you in establishing goals for your professional and personal growth along the path of your life.

### Step 1: Self-Reflection

One of the most effective ways to develop as a person is to practice self-reflection, which involves taking stock of your feelings, actions, and life experiences. Being more self-aware, emotionally intelligent, and knowledgeable about who you are can be achieved through purposeful self-reflection. When you reflect on yourself, you look closely at your fundamental principles and beliefs. You can make better decisions that are in line with your genuine selves if you take the time to figure out what is important and then act in a way that reflects these ideals. You can build a life with greater meaning, and fulfilment can be built around this alignment. Welcome the difficulties you have encountered and will encounter.

Additionally, it promotes being truthful about your abilities and areas for improvement. Gaining self-assurance and mastery via playing to your abilities is possible when you take the time to identify and appreciate them. At the same time, being honest about your shortcomings will also allow you to grow and improve because it will let you know where you may use some more work. Take the initiative by reflecting on your values, passions, and long-term vision. Reflect on the questions like *What truly matters to you? What do you aspire to achieve in different areas of your life—be it career, relationships, health, or personal development?* You will be able to comprehend more the facts of what you are and what you want to be.

### Step 2: SMART Goals Framework

SMART goals are Specific, Measurable, Achievable, Relevant, and Time-bound. This approach helps make goals SMART—Specific, Measurable, Achievable, Relevant, and Time-bound. This framework optimizes self-development by providing a clear path. The "S" in SMART stands for "Specific", emphasising the personal growth goals must be clear. For instance, instead of saying "improve communication skills," you could specify "attend a public speaking workshop to enhance communication skills." Measurable is SMART's "M".

Setting quantifiable goals helps you track and celebrate progress. Rather than "exercise regularly," try "exercise for at least 30 minutes five times a week." SMART's "A" means making goals achievable. Despite the need to push yourself, setting unrealistic goals might demoralize you. In SMART, the "R" stands for relevance, emphasizing aligning goals with larger goals and personal convictions. Goals should be meaningful and help you improve. This structure's "T" represents the requirement to set goals and deadlines. Without a schedule, goals may appear less urgent and progress slower. Communicating goals helps clarify ambitions. Measuring your progress will enhance your motivation and sense of accomplishment. Set realistic, achievable goals to avoid feeling overwhelmed and maintain a positive outlook. Be sure they are clear, quantitative, reasonable, linked with your values, and have a deadline.

### Step 3: Break Down Goals

Break larger goals into smaller, manageable tasks or milestones. Dissecting overarching goals into more achievable sub-goals is an important and smart step in your goal-setting for identifying self-development. This method improves understanding, makes it easier for you to plan, and encourages a systematic approach to achieving achievement. Many fields make use of the tried-and-true method of goal-breaking, including those dealing with organizational planning, project management, and personal growth. With its help, you will be able to identify your intended results with more clarity and precision. Team members or individuals might avoid confusion by breaking down overarching objectives into more manageable, particular sub-goals. With such clarity, the goals may be more easily identified, and the way ahead can be more easily navigated. When you set your sights too high, you risk becoming paralyzed by fear or doubt. Making things more feasible requires breaking them down into smaller, more doable tasks. By breaking down your big objectives into more manageable chunks, you will be able to make progress toward the larger objective.

It will also help you organize your time better. You will be able to make better use of your time and resources when you are well-known for your detailed task. Preventing procrastination and giving each work the attention it deserves within the overall timeframe are both achieved with this planned strategy. This breakdown makes goals more attainable and helps track progress effectively.

### Step 4: Prioritization and Focus

If you want to grow as a person in a meaningful and successful way, setting goals for yourself and sticking to them requires you to prioritize and concentrate. Being able to focus means devoting your time, effort, and resources to the most important goals, whereas being able to prioritize means recognizing and ranking goals according to their importance and effect. Knowing what you want out of life is the first step in creating a prioritized list. You can better understand your purpose if goals are defined in terms of precise and measurable outcomes. When you know what you want out of life and can put diverse objectives in perspective, you can prioritize them more effectively. Assessing the relevance and effect of every objective is also part of it. When it comes to developing your character, not all goals are created equal. Before deciding which goals to prioritize, consider how each one can affect your life, happiness, and long-term objectives. This will help you choose which goals are most in line with your values and vision. It entails arranging objectives in a rational sequence. Before or as a basis for additional objectives, you may need to complete some. By arranging your goals in a logical sequence, you will be confident that you will acquire the knowledge, experience, and credentials necessary to tackle more complex and challenging tasks. Efforts to better oneself are generally more fruitful when they are strategically sequenced. Make sure that you prioritize your goals based on importance and feasibility. Try focusing on a few key objectives to avoid spreading yourself too thin and maintain concentrated effort.

**Step 5: Visualize and Affirm**

Create visual representations of your goals in your mind, such as vision boards, or try written affirmations. By engaging in the mental exercise of visualization, you can imagine yourself accomplishing your objectives. It entails enveloping yourself in the sights, sounds, and feelings linked to your achievements and building a clear mental picture of the desired results. Your attitude, conduct, and performance can all be much improved with the help of this mental rehearsal.

Convince yourself that whenever I use visualization to help me grow personally, I make sure to picture every little detail of reaching my objectives. I picture myself succeeding at whatever goal I set for myself, whether it is reaching a professional milestone, improving my health habits, or becoming an expert in a new area. I envision myself boldly executing the required actions, triumphing over challenges, and relishing in the flavour of achievement. This mental picture gives me a clear and inspiring glimpse of the future I want to achieve. Remind yourself that by giving your dreams physical form in your imagination, visualization can boost your motivation. I envision myself participating in the necessary actions to attain achievement rather than only harbouring abstract ambitions. I am energized and focused as I continue my road of self-development, thanks to this mental rehearsal that provides a feeling of excitement and resolve. Visualizing your goals will reinforce commitment and enhance motivation.

**Step 6:  Regular Review and Adaptation**

Knowing the difference between a success list and a simple to-do list is a crucial part of goal setting. You have to see that certain points fall within the category of "to-do list," such as dinner, lunch, and tea break. On the other hand, our accomplishments may include working, reading, meeting, coming up with ideas, and many other things. You must give your daily success list your undivided attention. These pertain to objectives and aims. Things may not always go according to plan when you first begin implementing your day-to-day plans. You need to assess your progress and make adjustments based on your objectives during this time. Never lose sight of your end objective—just adjust your approach, if necessary. Adapt goals to changing circumstances while staying aligned with your overarching vision. Regularly review your goals. Start assessing your progress. Start celebrating your achievements and recalibrate

Keep in mind that goal setting is the compass that steers us towards self-actualization. By understanding the profound impact of setting meaningful goals and following a structured approach to define, refine, and pursue these objectives, you can embark on a purposeful journey toward personal growth and fulfilment.

# Chapter 3:
# Overcoming Challenges

*"The greater the obstacle, the more glory in overcoming it."*
*-Molière*

## Common Obstacles in Personal Growth

The act of embarking on a journey of personal growth is a courageous venture that carries the promise of enhanced resilience, increased self-discovery, and a more satisfying life. On the other hand, this path to transformation is not devoid of difficulties; indeed, you will frequently come across a plethora of obstacles that have the potential to hamper your development and put your dedication to change to the test. Although embarking on a road of self-development is a daring attempt, it is not without its share of difficulties. Some challenges appear along the way to advancement and self-development. There can be both internal and external barriers that can put your commitments and determinations to the test, not only for you but for anybody interested in cultivating personal development. It is necessary to not only comprehend but also successfully navigate these typical obstacles.

*"The best means of revenge is remaining professional and doing what is best for your career despite the actions you might encounter."*

## Some of the Common Challenges:

### Self-Doubt and Fear:

Fear and self-doubt can be your fiercest enemies when it comes to developing individually. They frequently operate as sneaky roadblocks that erode your self-assurance and prevent you from moving forward. These difficulties could crush your dreams, restrict your potential, and keep you from reaching your full potential.

Self-doubt can be an internal conflict that shows up as a lack of self-worth, ability, or decision-making confidence. It may have its roots in your negative self-comparisons, social expectations, or past failures.

Inner doubts and fears often hinder progress, causing hesitation and limiting beliefs. When self-doubt decays, it can make you mistrust your abilities, judgment, and general ability to accomplish your objectives. This widespread uncertainty has the potential to become a self-fulfiling prophecy that affects your actions and prevents you from pursuing possibilities for personal and self-development.

The comparison trap, in which you assess your value by comparing it to the accomplishments or standards of others, is one of the main sources of self-doubt. The tendency to measure oneself against carefully constructed representations of success can be especially strong in the modern day. You have to go past it. However, in contrast, fear and self-doubt are intimately related; fear frequently intensifies the feeling of uncertainty and trepidation that comes with personal development initiatives. Fear of not knowing what to do, of failing, or of being judged can be crippling; it keeps you from taking chances and moving beyond your comfort zone to further your personal development. This fear, which stems from your natural desire to protect yourself, can obstruct creativity, discovery, and the quest for new experiences that advance personal growth.

It will take a conscious effort on your part to identify and confront these negative thought patterns if you want to overcome fear and self-doubt. Developing self-awareness and recognizing your achievements and qualities are crucial stages in fortifying yourself against the damaging impacts of self-doubt.

**Procrastination and Lack of Discipline:**

Procrastination may have affected you in a variety of ways. The tendency to delay actions or lack consistent discipline can impede growth.

The persistent problem of procrastination, which involves putting off chores or avoiding important acts, can have an impact on many facets of your life. It frequently results from a confluence of elements, such as a lack of drive, a fear of failing, and the constant delaying from responsibilities. Procrastinators may discover that they give in to the temptation of transient pleasures or diversions, prioritizing their pursuit of short-term objectives over long-term objectives.

Perfectionism is a major cause of procrastination. It is the unachievable desire for perfection that might prevent you from starting work until you believe the conditions are perfect. The persistent procrastination that results from waiting for the "perfect" opportunity to start can be caused by the fear of not living up to unrealistic expectations.

You must adopt the idea that imperfect progress is still progressing to overcome this component of procrastination. Procrastination presents difficulties that are made worse by a lack of discipline. You must first determine the root causes of your procrastinating behaviour in order to overcome it and teach discipline. Having this self-awareness is essential to creating focused methods to deal with particular triggers. Additionally, you can use a good strategy to divide up more ambitious objectives into smaller, more doable tasks. This helps to decrease the perceived difficulty of a task and increases the likelihood of success. Make an organized plan and try to set reasonable timeframes. It might assist you in combating the inclination to put things off by offering a clear course of action.

**External Pressures and Criticism:**

Criticism and pressure from others can have a significant effect on your life, affecting your feelings, actions, and even your self-worth.

The way you react to these outside influences can have an important impact on your mental condition, personal development, and general level of contentment with life. External influences can have a big impact on you or anyone else. Society conventions, familial expectations, or cultural standards usually cause these pressures. People may comply with these external expectations out of a desire for acceptance and approval from others, sometimes at the expense of being true to who they truly are. In relationships, work, or personal accomplishments, the pressure to live up to specific standards can lead to feelings of inadequacy and an obsessive search for approval from others.

External influences can have an impact on more than just your conformity; they can also cause tension, worry, and a persistent sense of being watched. The overwhelming dread of not living up to expectations from others can prevent you from taking chances and following your actual passions and ideals. These stresses can build up over time and cause burnout, which can lower your general well-being and make it more difficult to pursue true personal fulfilment.

Likewise, helpful or not, criticism is another outside element that has the potential to have a big impact on others, including you. Unwarranted or harsh criticism can be emotionally exhausting, while constructive criticism can offer insightful information and growth opportunities. Your confidence and sense of self-worth can be affected by how you take criticism and handle it. External influences, societal norms, or criticism may sway us from our chosen path, so you must know how to work on them.

## Strategies for Overcoming Setbacks and Building Resilience

### Cultivating a Growth Mindset:

In general, there are two types of mindsets. Let's examine a fixed mindset first. When people adopt a fixed mindset, they see the quality of intelligence as innate and unchangeable over time. They focus a lot on their 'smart skills' and primarily on anything else they excel at. Conversely, they struggle with problems because it can indicate insufficiency or deficiencies or expose them to actual self-perception. Anyone with a fixed mindset lacks the motivation to take on challenges and frequently struggles with unpredictability because success is not guaranteed. Fixed mindset individuals are disciplined in believing they 'are who they are' and are consistently too uninspired to work hard.

Conversely, those who have a growth mindset have an incredibly different perspective. Teenagers who possess a growth mindset recognize that hard work can enhance and increase their aptitude and intelligence. They give learning a lot of weight and seem intelligent less of it. They take on obstacles as a chance to improve. Since their self-image is not based on insecurities, obstacles, failure, and the fear of making mistakes do not deter them. Their ideology dictates that they can win at anything.

Instead of having a fixed mindset, try adopting a growth mindset. Adopt a growth mindset. *Try viewing setbacks as opportunities for learning and growth rather than failures.* As mentioned in my TEDx talk, *"Failure is just the first step towards success."* Embrace challenges as stepping stones toward improvement. A growth mindset makes an effort to learn new things and develop your abilities. Negative comments and criticism can also be helpful tools for opening your eyes to new ideas. A growth attitude does not make people steel. Criticism can cause you some discomfort, but if the criticism relates to your abilities, you will be open to it because you will have that desire to embrace change and achieve your full potential. It will make you work more to obtain greater success, and when you do it well, you will be able to achieve what you desire.

### Self-Compassion and Acceptance:

Self-compassion and self-acceptance are two fundamental practices that can stand out as foundations of your emotional resilience and self-fulfilment in the complex fabric of your personal development and well-being. If you integrate these techniques into your everyday routine, they can have a beneficial and harmonious effect on your connection with yourself. The gentle art of treating oneself with the same love, understanding, and support that one would gladly provide to a dear friend is the foundation of self-compassion. You must consciously accept that you are a fallible, imperfect human being and that there will be obstacles and setbacks on your path. However, in contrast, attempt to recognize your goodness. That is yet another essential component of self-compassion. It is about giving yourself the comfort and support that you naturally provide to others when they are in need. It will promote a calming internal conversation when presented with challenges rather than giving in to self-criticism. Acknowledge imperfections and setbacks with kindness rather than harsh self-judgment.

Taking up self-compassion. Acknowledge that flaws and errors are a natural part of being human, and give yourself the grace to improve and learn. Self-acceptance is a powerful discipline that runs parallel to self-compassion. Accept yourself as you are, without criticism or the constant desire to get better. Recognize that your value is innate and unaffected by outside accomplishments or social norms. Acknowledge and accept your intrinsic value. Release yourself from the shackles of societal norms that frequently determine your perceived value and break free from the conditional aspect of self-worth. Regardless of any outside affirmation, unconditional self-acceptance and compassion will enable you to view yourself through a compassionate and loving lens.

### Goal Reevaluation and Adaptation:

Obstacles may be an unavoidable travelling partner as you pursue your career and personal objectives. When faced with challenges, it is not only necessary but also powerful to reevaluate your objectives and tactics and modify them to fit the constantly changing context of your situation. You can adjust your strategies or deadlines with this adaptable strategy, which is characterized by resilience and adaptability, without giving up on your overall goal.

When problems occur, the first action taken is frequently a critical turning point. When faced with challenges, reassess goals and strategies. You can adopt a mindset of re-evaluation in place of giving in to irritation or seeing challenges as insurmountable snags. This entails taking a critical, strategic look at your current objectives and processes to identify areas that could use improvement.

Modify approaches or timelines as needed without abandoning the overall vision. Reevaluating your objectives is the primary phase in this dynamic strategy. *Do they still fit in with your overall goal?* Conditions that change could require you to re-evaluate your goals or look for fresh chances that you were not aware of at first. Re-evaluating your goals allows you to stay flexible and sensitive to the changing environment. Think about adopting a flexible mentality. You can investigate different approaches, think of creative solutions, or incorporate new viewpoints from other people if you have an adaptable attitude. Try incorporating change into your objectives.

This adaptive process is a planned recalibration rather than a retreat from your overarching objective. Your dedication to your long-term goals and overarching purpose will not waver. This cyclical cycle of review and refinement will encourage adaptability and creativity, making sure that your path to success is marked by strategic flexibility as opposed to inaction.

**Developing Resilience through Adversity:**

Resilience is nurtured through adversity. Adversity is the furnace in which resilience, or the ability to overcome obstacles with greater vigour than before, is created. Embrace difficulties as opportunities to build resilience muscles. Consider challenges, disappointments, and hardships as chances to exercise and build your resilience rather than as barriers to success. When you accept adversity as a driving force behind your personal development, difficulties become worthwhile learning opportunities that are crucial to the formation of your resilience and inner fortitude.

When faced with challenges, cultivate resilience to shift your viewpoint. Adversity should be seen as a training field rather than an impassable barrier. Every adversity turns into a chance to build resilience, the mental and emotional toughness required to handle the challenges of everyday life.

Developing your resilience also requires you to ask for help when you need it. Seek support from mentors, friends, or communities during tough times. Human links, whether via groups, friends, or mentors, offer priceless resources. You can weather storms by asking for advice, asking others about their experiences, or just being there to encourage one another. The support you receive from these relationships serves as a cushion against life's obstacles, letting you know that you are not travelling alone.

Try seeking inspiration from mentors. Mentors can provide you with advice based on your personal experiences, offering you viewpoints and insights that can help you see the way ahead. Your friends can also help you emotionally by building a network of comprehension and support that enables you to build a collective resilience that will help you get through your challenges.

**Mindfulness and Stress Management:**

Incorporate mindfulness practices and stress management techniques to navigate challenging moments with clarity and composure. It will function as a strong remedy against the constant stress that comes with living in the modern world. Chronic stress can cause harm to your physical and mental health. The demands of your job, relationships, or outside factors can frequently cause it. By focusing attention on the present moment, mindfulness interrupts the autopilot mode that generates stress. It will make it possible for you to react to pressures more thoughtfully and in a more controlled manner.

Stress management approaches will offer a useful toolkit for competing the physiological and psychological effects of stress, which somebody can be used in conjunction with mindfulness. For example, deep breathing exercises trigger the body's relaxation response, which offsets the effects of the fight-or-flight reaction brought on by stress. By gradually tensing and then relaxing muscle groups, progressive muscle relaxation encourages physical relaxation that leads to a more tranquil state of mind. By developing mental discipline, meditation—whether it be mindfulness or focused attention—improves resilience to stress.

Including these routines in your daily life is a proactive approach to total well-being rather than just a crisis management strategy. Regular mindfulness practice will develop a resilience reservoir in you that will gradually change how you see and handle obstacles.

**Learn from Setbacks:**

Reflect on setbacks as lessons. Instead of viewing setbacks as roadblocks, we can view them as opportunities to uncover profound truths. Your ability to ponder and analyze is crucial when encountering a setback. Take a step back and examine the situation critically, looking closely at the facts and contributing variables. The goal of this reflective process is to gain important lessons from failure rather than to dwell on your failure. Examine what went wrong and glean insightful information to steer clear of the same mistakes in the future.

Understanding the dynamics at work better can be achieved by dissecting what went wrong. Name the precise factors that caused the setback. It will enable you to approach your progress in a focused and calculated manner. Understanding the underlying reasons is only one of the objectives; another is to identify trends and connections among different elements.

If you look at these failures through the prism of learning, they can become a wealth of knowledge. Gaining knowledge from failures will help to create a strategy that is more adaptable and robust. It is not just about avoiding similar mistakes in the future; it is also about actively using failures as steppingstones toward personal development and ongoing progress. By accepting failures as important teaching opportunities, you can turn misfortune into a driving force for advancement, equipped with the understanding to overcome obstacles in the path to further success.

### Persistence and Consistency:

Persist despite setbacks. Consistency in effort, even in small increments, can lead to your gradual progress. You may overcome obstacles in your path to success by being persistent and consistent. Persistence in the face of adversity is the unwavering resolve to move onward in the face of challenges and momentary setbacks. It is the ability to persevere in the face of difficulty and to turn failures into opportunities for growth and progress.

Persistence is enhanced by consistency, which is the unwavering commitment to a selected path of action. Consistency gives the trip a sense of predictability and dependability. Gradual growth is propelled forward by constant effort, even in the tiniest steps. It is the understanding that regular habits and small victories, as opposed to occasional spurts of action, are frequently the cause of success. Additionally, consistency can generate momentum, establishing a continuous rhythm that drives people toward their objectives with unwavering resolve. Persistence and consistency work together to create the foundation of success, turning goals into reality. Their mutually beneficial interaction makes sure that obstacles become chances for growth and learning, which eventually results in the accomplishment of long-term goals.

Challenges are not roadblocks but checkpoints in our self-development expedition. By employing strategies to confront obstacles head-on, cultivating resilience, and viewing setbacks as opportunities for self-development and growth, individuals can navigate the inevitable hurdles on the path to personal growth with grit and determination.

# Chapter 4:
# Building Positive Habits

*A habit cannot be tossed out the window; it must be coaxed down the stairs a step at a time. -Mark Twain*

## The Role of Habits in Shaping Our Lives

Habits are known as the invisible architects of our daily existence. It can wield immense power in shaping our behaviours, routines, and, ultimately, our lives. They define the fabric of our actions and contribute significantly to our overall well-being and success. Habits are in everyone's life. At this very moment, you are probably able to mention several of your own, some of which are nice and some of which are less than ideal, and things that you might want to change for the better. Because you have engaged in these actions so frequently, they have developed into a habit for you, even though you do not consciously think about engaging in them. Jogging, clapping, or giving someone a high-five when we are happy are all examples of habits. Habits are things that we do out of habit and without conscious thought. Our routines can bring about a significant change in our life. Just take a look at the things that we can achieve if we make this new habit a part of our routine.

People have a variety of habits. Because we are accustomed to things being done in a particular manner, it is quite challenging for us to venture outside of our comfort zone. It is a method that we are accustomed to, which is why we feel at ease with it. In other words, that is how a habit feels. It is necessary to alter your routines if you wish to bring about a shift in your life. Fortunately, once you have finished reading this chapter, you will be able to gain an understanding of how your habits function and how they will impact your development. It will be much simpler for you to develop new habits and maintain the ones you already have.

## Understanding Habit Formation:

Scientifically, the establishment of habits is fundamentally a neurological process that is hardwired into the brain's structure. Habit formation relies heavily on the basal ganglia, an area linked to motor control and procedural learning. Through regular practice, humans can automate previously learned behaviour by reinforcing brain circuits. As a result of this feedback loop in the nervous system, what starts as an intentional behaviour eventually becomes habitual.

But there are many other parts to habit formation beyond the neurological component. The idea of cue-routine-reward is deeply connected to habits from a psychological perspective. Charles Duhigg popularized this habit loop in his book "The Power of Habit," which lays out the essential steps in developing a habit. The cue acts as a habit trigger, telling the brain to start the routine, which is the actual behaviour. A positive consequence that supports the habit loop is the reward, which is, in turn, brought about by the routine. If you want to shape habits on purpose, you need to understand and control these factors.

What we have to know is that there is a substantial impact on the social and environmental settings where habits are developed. Societal standards can influence reinforcement or modification of habits, the actions of one's peers, and cultural expectations. Social modelling, in which people unknowingly imitate the actions of those around them, is a prime example of the pervasiveness of social influence. Depending on the behaviour being replicated, this process can either solidify existing habits or instigate new ones. Through consistent and repetitive actions, habits become deeply ingrained behaviours. Their influence on our actions and decisions is often subconscious as if they were running on autopilot. In my TEDx talk, I highlighted the importance of sticking to your decisions and not allowing others to sway your choices. Humans can have both good and negative habits. Maintaining positive habits can help us improve ourselves, while bad ones can hold us back. The actual issue arises when we become stuck in a repetitive pattern and fail to break free for personal progress. Breaking free from that cycle and the negative behaviours you have developed over the years will not be easy, no matter how much you strive. Habits are ingrained behaviours formed through repetition and consistency. They operate on autopilot, influencing our actions and decisions often without conscious thought.

## Impact of Habits:

### Routine and Efficiency:

A person's capacity for self-improvement is heavily impacted by their habits or the deeply embedded patterns of conduct that permeate their everyday life. Efficiency and regularity go hand in hand, and when you master both, you can shape your actions, thoughts, and approach to life in truly transformational ways. The force that shapes our lives is routine, which is frequently linked with the ordinary and the boring. The regularity with which one goes about one's everyday activities provides a foundation upon which one can build one's development. Positive habits have an outsized effect on one's development and progress in life. Imagine your morning routine as a deliberate choice to rise at a certain hour, do things that feed your mind and body, and establish a routine for the day. This seemingly insignificant pattern will lay the groundwork for a more disciplined and organized life. It will encourage people to think ahead and approach each day with purpose. You will find more stability in life as a result. It takes deliberate action to interrupt the current pattern and introduce new, positive habits that are in line with personal objectives and advancements if you want to break free from your harmful patterns.

Meanwhile, being efficient in one's development means knowing how to put one's time and effort to good use. Staying focused on your objectives and approaching chores and activities strategically are essential. Think about the process of acquiring a new ability. Embracing efficiency means figuring out what works best for learning, making the most of what we have, and cutting out what does not. Your capacity to precisely plan for and complete tasks is a characteristic of your efficient habits.

**Behaviour Reinforcement:**

Reinforcement is a technique that has its origins in the concepts of behaviorism. It involves the utilization of either positive or negative stimuli in order to enhance or weaken a certain behavior of yours for your development. Reinforcement tactics have the potential to mold your habits, encourage positive changes in your life, and contribute to your long-term personal development when they are employed consciously within the context of self-improvement. Positive reinforcement, which comprises providing a favorable stimulus, can be used to motivate a desired behaviour in oneself. When it comes to the process of self-improvement, this can be a very helpful instrument for improving one's good behaviours and routines. For instance, if the objective is to build a pattern of daily exercise, one might act as a kind of positive reinforcement by rewarding oneself with a small treat or a minute of relaxation after completing a workout. To reinforce the intended action, it is essential to establish a connection between the desired behaviour and the pleasant stimulus, so producing a feeling of reward and satisfaction. You have to reinforce certain behaviours, whether positive or negative, by becoming ingrained in your subconscious.

## Practical Advice on Developing and Maintaining Positive Habits

To go on the road of self-improvement and personal growth, it is necessary to cultivate positive habits that are in alignment with your goals, values, and development. This is because the trip requires more than just personal aspirations. The way to transformation is frequently filled with obstacles although everyone shares the desire for positive change. When it comes to building and keeping excellent habits, this is when guidance that is both practical and helpful becomes valuable. Now, we will delve into a blueprint for enduring change, drawing on practical ideas to guide you through the process of habit-building and sustainability.

### Identify Keystone Habits:

The term "keystone habits" refers to actions that, when developed regularly, have the potential to have a domino effect on a variety of facets of your life. Attempt to form routines that can be beneficial to your personal growth and development. Identify key habits that can act as catalysts for other positive changes. For instance, you can establish a significant keystone habit by engaging in regular physical activity. The benefits of exercise extend far beyond the obvious physical benefits; it also has a significant influence on mental well-being, levels of discipline, and levels of vitality. Increasing your focus, improving your mood, and improving your general health are all benefits that may be achieved by maintaining a regular exercise regimen. This discipline will also tend to leak over into other aspects of your life, such as your work or personal pursuits, so laying the groundwork for your success.

One more essential routine is the ability to manage one's time effectively. Not only can the cultivation of habits linked to planning, prioritization, and goal setting help to enhance productivity, but it also contributes to a sense of purpose and accomplishment. How time is spent on various activities will be influenced by this habit, which will result in increased efficiency and the creation of space for both personal and professional development.

Another essential habit that serves as a cornerstone is the practice of mindfulness and contemplation. Meditation and introspection are two ways to establish a habit of mindfulness that can help you become more self-aware and emotionally intelligent. Your ability to make decisions on purpose, your ability to reduce stress, and your ability to have a better grasp of your personal beliefs will all be enhanced by adhering to this habit.

In addition, learning constantly and continuing your education can be a foundational habit that can have a profound impact on your life. It is possible to cultivate adaptability, resilience, and a growth mindset by committing to acquiring new knowledge and abilities. Your personal and professional lives will be enriched as a result of this habit, which will propel you beyond the boundaries of your comfort zones and so open doors to new chances. Focusing on these keystone habits can create a domino effect in transforming other areas of life.

**Start Small and Specific:**

It is possible to feel overwhelmed when beginning the process of habit development, particularly when one is confronted with lofty goals. One of the most attractive aspects of beginning with a small scale is that it can help alleviate the daunting nature of large changes. Initiate habit formation by starting small and being specific. Break down larger habits into manageable tasks to make them more achievable.

The process can be made more approachable by breaking the desired behaviour down into digestible, bite-sized components. This is preferable to the alternative of trying a drastic transformation.

For instance, if the objective is to establish a habit of reading, one way to begin would be to commit to reading just one page every day. The apparent amount of work and time commitment is reduced as a result of this low demand, which makes it easier to incorporate successfully into daily life. It is possible for you to progressively increase the reading objective as the habit becomes more established, thereby creating momentum over time.

The concept of micro-habits, which are little, easily attainable activities that serve as the building blocks for larger habits, can also be leveraged by beginning with a small amount of activity. A footing is established in your routine through the implementation of these micro-habits, which lays the groundwork for the development of more substantial habits in the times to come. The incremental approach is consistent with the idea that relatively minor adjustments made regularly can result in major outcomes over the long term.

**Consistency and Repetition:**

The foundation of habit formation is consistent practice. Consistent practice is crucial for habit formation. Doing anything regularly—ideally in the same setting and at the same time—requires a steadfast resolve. Consistency tells the brain that the action is meaningful, which encourages the formation of connections between brain regions that are normally unrelated to the habit. Psychologists have identified the cue-response-reward loop as a crucial component of habit formation, and consistency serves to reinforce the desired behaviour while simultaneously reinforcing it.

Conversely, habits are formed in daily routines through the process of repetition. When it comes to developing habits, the old saying "practice makes perfect" is correct. When we do something over and over again, it eventually becomes second nature and needs little to no thought on our part. Repetition reinforces behaviours, gradually embedding them into our daily routine.

Not only does repetition help with self-development, but it also reinforces the neurological connections linked to the habit. Keep your attention focused on reiterating these two essential components. The principles of behavioural psychology are in harmony with the power of repetition and consistency. Consistent reinforcement over time is the key to making a behaviour habitual, according to psychologists. When we do something over and over again, it becomes second nature, and we do not have to think about it as much.

**Trigger and Routine:**

Associate new habits with existing triggers or routines. One strategy that can help us incorporate more positive behaviours into our daily lives is to connect new habits to things that already happen to us, like triggers or routines. Making new habits into established behaviours makes their integration smoother. Making new habits easier to adopt and strengthening the interconnectedness of our routines, this approach takes advantage of the power of association and habit stacking.

A person's already established habits can serve as signals to start a new habit. The brain pathways already connected with an established behaviour can be used to help individuals form new habits when they intentionally pair them with existing routines. Aligning the process of making morning coffee with the objective of including a regular stretching regimen, for instance, generates a natural relationship.

The brain is signalled to begin the subsequent behaviour of stretching by the start of the day. In addition, a built-in reminder system is created by linking new behaviours to preexisting triggers. There is less chance of forgetfulness or negligence due to the built-in cues in established routines. To consistently remind oneself to write reflectively before bed, one could, for example, combine the practice of daily journaling at the end of the day.

**Accountability and Tracking:**

Try maintaining accountability by tracking your progress. If you are having trouble reinforcing good habits, try keeping a journal. Use an app to track. These tools will provide you with a visual depiction of your progress to monitor consistency and stay motivated.

You can benefit from habit-tracking applications in this regard. When it comes to bettering oneself, habit-tracking applications are now indispensable. Meditation and introspection are two ways to establish a habit of mindfulness that can help you become more self-aware and emotionally intelligent. These applications will provide an easy and accessible way to keep yourself accountable, whether it is by recording your workout routines, water intake, or reading habits. It will motivate you to maintain their routines.

Furthermore, it may be beneficial to maintain a journal. A more personal and reflective approach to monitoring your development is to keep a journal. As a bonus, keeping a journal can help you become more self-aware and provide light on how habits are formed. In addition to tracking your progress over time, writing down your routines can be a great source of inspiration.

The use of accountability partners makes habit tracking more social. Having someone you trust, such as a family member, mentor, or friend, to share your objectives and progress with builds a support system that keeps you committed. Individuals commit not just to themselves, but also to their accountability partners when they engage in regular check-ins and shared accountability, which in turn fosters a sense of responsibility.

### Focus on Behaviour, Not Outcome:

Focus on how you acted instead of what happened. Changing your behaviour regularly causes you to create habits that last, which in turn produces the desired results. The idea that long-term transformation requires a chain reaction of incremental improvements is consistent with this strategy. A new habit can take root and flourish when we consistently work to alter our behaviour in such a way that it becomes second nature. By highlighting the habit, people can recognize and value the small steps taken daily, which strengthens the link between their activities and the results they achieve.

While results are crucial, they are often the unintended consequence of doing something regularly. Throughout their continuous journey, individuals can achieve their intended objectives by focusing on building positive habits, which create a foundation for long-term improvement.

### Embrace Slip-ups with Compassion:

On the road to habit formation, you can anticipate obstacles and mistakes. To create habits, you must be prepared to face obstacles and make mistakes. Recognizing that difficulties are inevitable will empower you to face them with self-compassion and resilience, turning failures into chances for growth instead of reasons to give up. In my TEDx talk, I emphasized that while giving up may seem like the easiest option, it should never be the choice we make. Instead, we should strive to try harder and persevere, never giving up on our goals and aspirations.

Always keep in mind that experiencing setbacks is a normal part of going through a transformation. Due to the ever-changing nature of life, unexpected events or brief disruptions to the usual routine are inevitable. Acknowledging this innate uncertainty can empower you to confront obstacles with a caring frame of mind. Take a compassionate approach to these instances and view them as chances to learn, not as reasons to give up.

Reframe setbacks as opportunities for learning and development rather than setbacks themselves. Having a growth mindset means you may look at setbacks not as conclusions but as stepping stones on the path to success. If you can change your perspective and see obstacles as merely temporary impediments on the way to success, you will be more motivated to keep going. In addition to helping, you build habits, it will strengthen your resilience and adaptability, which are crucial for overcoming obstacles.

Always acknowledge that your positive habits serve as the cornerstone of your personal growth and success. By understanding the mechanisms behind habit formation and implementing practical strategies that focus on consistency, specificity, and incremental progress, individuals can cultivate positive habits that enrich their lives and lead to long-term positive change.

# Chapter 5:
# Mindfulness and Emotional Intelligence

*What matters is hard work, and emotional intelligence.*
*– Mickey Drexler*

Let's talk about the role of mentality, mindfulness, and emotional intelligence. Many people in today's fast-paced society feel disconnected, worried, and overwhelmed. Anxiety, despair, and burnout can result from the continual barrage of information, distractions, and demands we face. We can overcome the challenges of modern life and learn to find happiness and peace within ourselves by practising mindfulness. Mindfulness and emotional intelligence are pillars of personal growth, fostering profound self-awareness and enriching our interactions with the world. They empower us to navigate life's complexities with clarity and empathy.

## Mindfulness:

To triumph over the challenges of contemporary living and discover inner happiness and tranquility, we must grasp the concept of mindfulness. Practising mindfulness is essential for realizing how fleeting and interdependent everything is. Things become more apparent for what they truly are: fleeting as we learn to observe our experiences without passing judgment. Every aspect of our being, from ideas and feelings to bodily sensations, is transient and subject to change. As we train our minds to be more present, we also start to notice how everything is related. Every moment is interwoven with every other moment in the vast tapestry of existence, and we come to understand this. All living things are interrelated, and human activities have consequences for the environment. Mindfulness is the practice of being present and attentive to our thoughts, emotions, and surroundings without judgment.

## How mindfulness can help you:

### Reduced Stress:

Mindfulness techniques alleviate stress by promoting a focus on the present moment. Being attentive means focusing your attention on the here and now, judgment-free. By encouraging people to notice their thoughts and feelings without getting caught up in them, this practice clears the mind and makes it possible to react to stressors with greater consideration and moderation. Stress is frequently caused by cycles of ruminating on the past or worrying about the future, which can be broken by developing a nonjudgmental awareness of the present. Try utilizing methods that are associated with mindfulness. Mindfulness-based meditation is one option. This important technique involves either guided or unguided meditation sessions that teach individuals how to notice their thoughts and feelings without responding to them. This will lessen the negative effects of pressures on mental health by fostering a sense of clarity and serenity.

Regular mindfulness practice has been repeatedly linked to several advantages, such as lowered stress levels, happier moods, and increased resilience in general. By integrating mindfulness into everyday activities, people may better handle the ups and downs of life with more composure, which promotes balance and serenity in the face of the fast-paced, modern world.

### Improved Mental Clarity:

With origins in ancient contemplative traditions, mindfulness has been the focus of a lot of interest lately because of its remarkable capacity to enhance mental clarity in contemporary circumstances. Fundamentally, mindfulness is the deliberate practice of cultivating awareness in the here and now, urging people to notice their thoughts without passing judgment. It enhances mental clarity and concentration, aiding in decision-making and problem-solving. This technique offers a road to mental clarity through focused attention, which acts as a potent counterbalance to the din of distractions in our everyday lives.

You can learn to free yourself from the web of recurring ideas that frequently clog your mental spaces by spractising mindfulness. Clarity might arise from this purposeful, impartial study of your thoughts. Additionally, the exercise will strengthen one's ability to focus attention on the present moment and foster a deeper sense of concentration. In addition to improving focus and cognitive abilities, this also helps with heightened attention, contributing to overall mental acuity.

However, mindfulness is also very useful in reducing stress and anxiety, which are frequent obstacles to mental clarity. You can also learn how to react to challenges with grit and poise by spractising regularly. Stress reduction will help you achieve mental calmness, which will further improve your ability to think clearly.

### Enhanced Emotional Regulation:

For those aiming for a stable and well-rounded emotional existence, mindfulness is a guiding light due to its significant influence on emotional control. Mindfulness cultivates the ability to observe emotions without reacting impulsively. Cultivating a nonjudgmental awareness of the current moment, including one's thoughts and feelings, is the fundamental component of mindfulness. Through this practice, you will be able to become more attuned to your emotional states without giving in to reactive habits. Observing emotions without passing judgment on them will help you gain a deeper comprehension and acceptance of them.

By encouraging a pause between input and response, mindfulness improves emotional regulation in several important ways. You will be able to resist the need to react rashly in the face of emotional stimuli by making this space for deliberate thinking. The foundation of emotional intelligence is this deliberate pause, which helps you handle difficult situations with more poise.

Additionally, mindfulness encourages an attitude of emotional detachment—not in a repressive way, but rather in a way that lets you feel your feelings without becoming consumed by them. Having the capacity to keep a balanced viewpoint on emotions would undoubtedly help one's emotional state become steadier.

**The connection between mindfulness and emotional intelligence:**

A high level of emotional intelligence is characterized by self-awareness, social awareness, and emotional regulation skills. Having this skill is crucial in any connection, whether it is personal or professional. Because it trains one to pay closer attention to and control one's feelings, mindfulness is a potent technique for emotional intelligence development. Here, we will delve into how mindfulness can help you become more emotionally intelligent, how to cultivate mindfulness to boost your emotional intelligence, and how it can alleviate stress and make you more resilient.

**Emotional Intelligence:**

Emotional intelligence encompasses understanding, managing, and leveraging emotions effectively.

Understanding, managing, and effectively utilizing one's own and other people's emotions are only a few examples of the many facets that make up emotional intelligence. A key notion in leadership, interpersonal interactions, psychology, and emotional intelligence was popularized by novelist Daniel Goleman and coined by psychologists John Mayer and Peter Salovey.

The core of emotional intelligence is the capacity to recognize, comprehend, and regulate one's own emotions. To properly identify your emotions and comprehend the elements impacting them, you must possess this essential component of self-awareness. It requires a sophisticated comprehension of the intricate relationship between feelings and ideas, and it is beyond mere emotional awareness. Emotional intelligence's second component is the ability to identify and understand others' feelings.

The ability to read and respond to the emotional cues of people around you is a key component of strong relationships and fruitful dialogue. Being empathetic is more than just being able to identify your own emotions; it also means being able to put yourself in another person's shoes and comprehend their thoughts and feelings. The capacity to control and direct one's emotional responses is the subject of emotional regulation, the third facet of emotional intelligence.

Emotionally intelligent people can handle the highs and lows of their emotions without losing control. Among these abilities is the ability to control one's emotions and express them appropriately in various settings. Taken as a whole, emotional intelligence serves as a comprehensive framework that includes motivation, social skills, emotional regulation, empathy, and self-awareness. This framework significantly impacts how you navigate the complexity of your feelings and relate to other people.

Emotional intelligence is a dynamic and teachable skill set that may help you grow personally, lead effectively, and build more harmonious and fruitful connections in both your personal and professional life. Emotional intelligence bestows many advantages in personal, social, and professional spheres, enhancing overall success and well-being.

Here are a few main benefits:

**Improved Relationships:**

High emotional intelligence fosters better communication and empathy in relationships. Better empathy and communication in relationships are fostered by high emotional intelligence. Being able to perceive and comprehend your feelings is a sign of having high emotional intelligence, which allows you to express yourself honestly. Being able to express your emotions comes from having self-awareness, which is the cornerstone of good communication. A deeper connection can be forged, and sympathetic reactions can be facilitated by people with high emotional intelligence's ability to recognize others' feelings.

If you have high emotional intelligence, you can handle delicate situations and disagreements with poise and create a more peaceful atmosphere by controlling your own emotions. You can establish a sympathetic and discerning dynamic in relationships by actively listening, validating emotions, and responding with empathy. In general, emotional intelligence strengthens the emotional bonds between people and encourages open communication, understanding, and interpersonal skills. A more robust bond can be achieved in partnerships when partners can sensitively manage their emotions.

**Enhanced Self-Awareness:**

It promotes a deeper understanding of one's emotions and their impact on actions. Focusing on self-awareness and self-regulation, it encourages greater knowledge of emotions and how they affect behavior. Proficient in identifying and categorizing their feelings, as well as picking out subtleties in their emotional terrain, are people with high emotional intelligence. Their increased self-awareness enables individuals to comprehend the underlying reasons for their emotions and the potential behavioural effects of those feelings.

Furthermore, efficient emotion regulation is a component of emotional intelligence. As a result, you can avoid making rash decisions motivated by intense feelings by learning to regulate and control your emotional reactions. Those with high emotional intelligence can gain a comprehensive understanding of the relationship between emotions and actions through introspection and mindfulness. It will help you make more deliberate and thoughtful decisions, which will promote your development and improve the calibre of your relationships with other people. It is useful for navigating the intricate relationship between feelings and actions, which will help you take more deliberate actions.

Let me share my personal experience with you, which I have also talked about in my TEDx talk:

There was a friend of mine who was like a sister to me, we both attended the same university. I had plans to obtain my master's degree earlier than usual. After she came to know about it, she began to discourage me, often coming up with excuses. As the time passed, our relationship deteriorated. We both started looking for jobs after graduation. I began applying everywhere, hoping to work for a multinational company. When she found out about my aspirations for such a job, she called me and tried to discourage me, saying that those positions require a lot of work.

After these incidents, I began to feel that she did not want what was best for me and might even be jealous of my success. Consequently, I decided to maintain a more casual relationship with her. This experience taught me to carefully consider decisions and not let anyone influence my choices once I have made them.

**Effective Conflict Resolution:**

Emotional intelligence aids in navigating conflicts by understanding diverse perspectives. Through the development of an awareness of many points of view, emotional intelligence is essential for managing disputes. Being able to identify and control one's emotions improves one's ability to empathize with others. When it comes to disagreements, people with high emotional intelligence are adept at reading the feelings and opinions of all parties involved. Communication and problem-solving skills improve with this understanding.

The ability to control one's own emotions helps people avoid impulsive behaviours that could worsen interpersonal conflicts. They are also capable of handling disagreements cooperatively by looking for points of agreement and coming up with solutions that consider different viewpoints. Emotional intelligence is a useful tool for dispute resolution and building healthy relationships in both the personal and professional domains because it fosters empathy and effective communication.

## Exercises to Enhance Self-Awareness and Empathy

### Mindful Breathing Exercise:

Practice deep breathing techniques to anchor yourself in the present moment. Conscious breathing is one of the popular methods. Focusing on the in and out breath is an important part of this practice. By bringing our attention to the breath, we can ground ourselves in the here and now and develop inner peace and insight. Focus on the inhalation and exhalation, allowing thoughts to pass without judgment.

### Body Scan Meditation:

Body scan meditation involves detecting and releasing tension from different body areas. Body awareness and relaxation improve with this activity. Sit or lie in a quiet place to start a body scan meditation. Close your eyes and deep breathing to center yourself. Focus from the top of your head down to each body part.

Pay attention to tension or discomfort without judgment. Release any stress after focusing on each part. Imagine that worry melts away as you breathe deeply and slowly. Witness your natural breath and body sensations. Increased body awareness promotes focus and relaxation. Finally, allow yourself to feel more serenity and connection with your body as you slowly open your eyes and end the meditation.

### Emotional Journaling:

Maintain an emotional journal to track and explore your feelings. Reflect on the triggers and patterns behind various emotions to foster deeper self-awareness. First, choose a peaceful place to sit comfortably. Then, practice gratitude and compassion meditation to cultivate empathy and positive feelings. Establish a composed mindset by starting with your breath. Focus on the aspects of your life that you are grateful for to begin with. Concentrate your mind on individuals, events, or features that make you feel thankful. Relish the feelings these ideas evoke.

Give yourself and others warmth and understanding as you shift to a compassion-focused meditation practice. Visualize your family, friends, and even those with whom you may have difficulties. Send them peaceful thoughts and best wishes for happiness and health.

**Active Listening Practice:**

Practice active listening in conversations—focus on understanding rather than immediately responding. Reflect on the speaker's emotions and thoughts to cultivate empathy. Prioritize comprehension over a quick reply when engaging in conversation to demonstrate active listening. Concentrate fully on the speaker, maintain eye contact, and avoid external distractions. While they are speaking, refrain from passing judgment and avoid prematurely thinking about your response.

Allocate more attention to understanding their feelings and ideas. To assure accuracy and demonstrate empathy, repeat back what you have heard. When indicating interest, use phrases like "I understand" or "It sounds like..." Be attentive to non-verbal cues such as body language and tone, in addition to spoken words. Even if you disagree, respect their viewpoint and validate their emotions. Empathy is cultivated through feeling heard and understood. Wait for the speaker to finish before responding with your thoughts. Active listening builds rapport and encourages open conversation by fostering a compassionate and understanding environment.

**Perspective-Taking Exercise:**

Imagine situations from different perspectives. This exercise builds empathy by encouraging an understanding of varied viewpoints and emotions. Even walking can help you regularly. Walking mindfully entails tuning into the bodily sensations experienced by the walker, such as the sensation of gravity and the swaying of the legs. Paying close attention to these feelings helps us stay in the here and now and develops a sense of steadiness and stability.

**Meditation:**

You can develop non-reactive awareness by curiously observing your thoughts and emotions during meditation. Introspection helps you identify your triggers and prejudices, boosting emotional intelligence. Your ability to empathize with others increases as you become more aware of their experiences and viewpoints.

It regulates emotions, calming and lowering your tension. This emotional equilibrium improves relationships and makes people more sympathetic and caring.

Mindfulness and emotional intelligence are transformative tools that enrich our lives. By embracing exercises that enhance self-awareness, empathy, and emotional regulation, individuals can embark on a journey towards greater emotional intelligence, fostering stronger relationships and a deeper understanding of themselves and the world around them

# Chapter 6:
# Cultivating Gratitude

*"Live in the sunshine, swim the sea, drink the wild air."*
*– Ralph Waldo Emerson*

Gratitude acts as a powerful elixir. Many of us do not know what the future holds, but we do know that we are living through historic, defining times. But change is on the way, so now is a good moment to assess our life goals and the resilience we will need to overcome obstacles. It does not matter where you are; you should know that being grateful is the easiest and most effective way to fight melancholy, anxiety, negativity, and physical or mental problems. *You need to make expressing gratitude for life a habit, just like learning to write well or excelling in school.* An increasing number of people in our modern day are undoubtedly realizing the therapeutic effect of thankfulness. Because of this, you will be able to turn obstacles into possibilities.

The rationality of the fact that one cannot be thankful and hostile (or furious, sad, or discouraged) simultaneously is becoming apparent to humanity. A spirit of gratitude fosters rest, contentment, and happiness. It promotes kindness, tolerance, and forgiveness. This is the way that will allow us to take advantage of the positive things happening in our lives. It enriches our lives and nurtures a positive mindset. Its influence extends beyond mere appreciation, shaping our perspectives and enhancing overall wellbeing.

## Benefits of Gratitude:

### Mental Health Boost:

Experiencing gratitude entails recognizing and cherishing all of life's blessings, no matter how minor. Intentionally focusing on your blessings sets off a series of beneficial psychological and physiological responses in you. Gratitude is linked to reduced stress, increased happiness, and improved mental resilience. The decrease in your stress levels is one of the noticeable effects. Refocusing your attention from what is lacking or difficult to what is there positively balances out the stress reaction. This change in viewpoint helps you maintain a more resilient and balanced mental state, enabling you to handle pressures better.

Furthermore, a stronger correlation has been shown between gratitude and happiness. Your general mood improves when you force yourself to participate in the practice of expressing and acknowledging thankfulness regularly. This emotionally beneficial effect is long-lasting and helps to maintain a feeling of wellbeing. Moreover, gratitude promotes a happier and more positive mindset by acting as a regular reminder of the good things in your life.

Developing an attitude of thankfulness might help you become mentally resilient during difficult circumstances. It will provide you with a coping strategy that works through obstacles. You can face challenges with more perspective and inner strength if you concentrate on your blessings. Resilience is the ability to confront issues with a more upbeat and hopeful perspective rather than diminishing or denying them.

**Enhanced Relationships:**

Gratitude strengthens bonds and promotes kindness, empathy, and reciprocity in relationships. It fosters stronger connections by encouraging compassion, kindness, and a sense of reciprocity. A positive feedback loop from showing appreciation, whether verbally or through action, strengthens relationships.

Thankfulness requires acknowledging others' kindness, contributions, and good qualities. Expressing your thankfulness goes beyond merely performing a good deed. It signifies excellent value. Acknowledging others fosters empathy because you become more aware of their feelings and thoughts. Sharing emotions strengthens relationships by improving mutual understanding.

An appreciative relationship fosters gratitude. Expressing gratitude or highlighting the good things that someone has done creates an atmosphere in which being kindness becomes a commodity that is exchanged. Experiencing gratitude can motivate you to make constructive contributions to the welfare of others, starting a positive feedback loop that improves the standard of your relationships. Consequently, this benevolence will enhance feeling of unity and mutual compassion.

Another essential component of gratitude is reciprocity, which creates a give-and-take dynamic that strengthens bonds with others. Expressing gratitude triggers a natural desire to receive it again, starting a positive feedback cycle of appreciation. This interchange is not transactional; it comes from a sincere desire to improve the relationship and fortify the emotional ties that bind people together.

It also acts as a potent counterbalance to negativity and interpersonal strife. People can face obstacles with a more balanced viewpoint if they concentrate on the positive and appreciated aspects of life. Disagreements are tackled with a foundation of understanding and generosity. This upbeat viewpoint contributes to a more robust and healthier marital dynamic.

**Physical Health Benefits:**

Extensive studies have shown that being grateful has numerous beneficial physiological effects, highlighting its power to improve one's wellbeing. Grateful individuals often experience better sleep, lower blood pressure, and a stronger immune system.

An increase in quality of sleep is one of the most obvious positive effects of appreciation on physical health. You can lessen the chances of insomnia and increase the likelihood of a good night's sleep by practising gratitude in the hours leading up to bedtime. A good night's sleep is best achieved when one is relaxed and content, both of which can be fostered through practising gratitude.

Additionally, there is evidence that being grateful might reduce blood pressure, which has positive effects on cardiovascular health. Noticing and enjoying the good things in life has a direct effect on lowering stress and increasing relaxation. The subsequent reduction in the likelihood of cardiovascular problems is a result of this, contributing to the preservation of normal blood pressure levels.

**Exercises for Cultivating Gratitude in Daily Life**

Regularly practising gratitude can have several beneficial impacts on one's mental and emotional health, and these consequences can be felt in a variety of ways. To assist in the development of a grateful mindset, the following are some acts that should be performed consistently:

**1. Write down your thoughts:**

Writing down your thoughts and feelings of gratitude for the good things in your life is a profound and life-altering activity. Regularly write down things you are grateful for—whether it is small moments, experiences, or people who positively impact your life. Keeping a thankfulness diary can be a great way to record the little things that make life worth living, the big events that matter, and the thoughts and feelings that you want to bring to your personal growth when you take some time to reflect. Reflect on why these things are meaningful to you. The mundane takes on new significance in this realm, where the extraordinary meets the everyday. The goal of this exercise is to help you become more attuned to the little details of your day that could otherwise slip your attention.

Listing your possessions is just the beginning; you must delve further into self-reflection to uncover the true essence of your admiration. A story of significance and connection is told in each entry. A tangible chronicle of positives will emerge from your journal as entries accumulate over time. When you are going through tough times, reading this book will give you the strength to keep going and show you that there are good things in life, even when things seem hopeless. By looking back, you can see the threads of thankfulness that run through your life, which can help you stay strong and optimistic.

Seeking and enjoying the wonderful things in life is a commitment. As a result, you start to see more of what you already have rather than what you may be missing. If you do this regularly, you can open yourself up to a world of possibilities, grow as a person, discover delight in the mundane, and cultivate an attitude of thankfulness that will impact every facet of your life.

**2. Being thankful:**

Continuously being thankful is an effective way to develop an optimistic outlook and a sense of gratitude. Begin your morning by being thankful for having another day and recognizing all the opportunities and possibilities it presents. Take time to appreciate the little things in life, like the comfort of a restful night's sleep or the sun's warmth.

Spend some time appreciating the day's experiences, whether big or small. Be thankful for the good times, the successes, and the knowledge gained. Acknowledge the assistance you have received from others and the difficulties that have given you the chance to improve.

Maintaining a gratitude notebook can help you remember your blessings and cultivate an attitude of thankfulness. When you regularly participate in these routines, your outlook will change, promoting resilience and a higher level of satisfaction in the morning and at night. As a conscious practice, gratitude prayers help you stay positive and improve your general well-being by aligning your attitude.

### 3. Gratitude Letters or Notes:

Write letters of gratitude to those who have made a difference in your life. Express your appreciation for their support, guidance, or kindness. Whether they are written or received, thank-you cards or letters are effective ways to show someone how much you value your relationship with them. These sincere comments are not just courteous; they are expressions of profound gratitude for the positive influence someone has had on the recipient's life.

Expressing gratitude turns these letters into poignant mementos of moments spent together, expressing gratitude for the support, advice, or generosity of the recipient. They serve proof of the importance of interpersonal relationships and the significant impact people can have on one another. Writing a letter of thanks is a therapeutic exercise that fosters attention and introspection. It is more than just a gesture. Give yourself time to feel incredibly grateful for all that you have done to influence my life. Tell them how their constant compassion, support, and advice have aided in your personal and professional development. Inform them how their support during difficult times has given you resilience and strength. Their astute advice has served as a compass, providing you more clarity and direction as you navigate life's challenges. Express how much you appreciate them and how their influence has transformed your life. Express your gratitude to them for being an inspiration and a guiding light in your journey for personal growth.

Acknowledged that cultivating gratitude is a transformative practice that elevates our wellbeing and enriches our experiences. By incorporating simple yet impactful exercises into daily life, individuals can harness the profound benefits of gratitude, fostering a positive outlook and deeper appreciation for life's blessings.

# Chapter 7:
# Effective Communication

*"Communication is the solvent of all problems and is the foundation for personal development."*

*– Peter Shepherd, psychologist, author*

Now let's have a look at how important it is to communicate well to advance personally and professionally. One very important tool is communication. Either way, it can improve or degrade our relationships. We talk to each other every day, practically everywhere, and always. While working, we converse with a variety of people, including our friends, family, coworkers, clients, and acquaintances. What counts is how we communicating with these people and how we receive their responses. The people we spend time with as friends, the places we enjoy visiting, the way we dress, and even the jobs we do all serve to tell people about who we are and who we are not.

## Ask yourself, "ARE YOU A GOOD COMMUNICATOR?"

Have those around you ever voiced complaints about your lack of communication? Do people understand you when you explain things to them? Without question, many people struggle with effective communication. Remember that mastering both verbal and nonverbal communication is a must for good communication.

## The Importance of Clear and Empathetic Communication

Clear and empathetic communication is the main aspect of healthy relationships, fostering understanding, trust, and connection. It is a dynamic skill set that goes beyond words, encompassing both verbal and non-verbal cues. People will not be able to complete tasks on their own, as numerous experts have already stated. They depend on other people to assist them in some manner because of this. Without purposefully asking for assistance, you cannot expect others to assist you. Make sure they understand what you need from them, why you are asking for their assistance specifically, and how they can support you in your communication with them.

Always keep in mind that you are not contacting others only to solicit assistance. In most cases, we speak with others to build relationships. Essentially, this means that if we can communicate successfully with others, we can create stronger social bonds with them. Ever questioned why two people cannot seem to get along? This is due to their realization that they lack a basis to initiate, let alone develop, a dialogue. Even in the same environment, they experience the feeling of being on two distinct planets. Communication is most effective when two people can fully comprehend one another and have topics of conversation in common. It really is crucial.

An individual will be unable to express himself clearly enough for others to comprehend him if he lacks acceptable communication abilities. A person's ability to articulate an idea clearly and with confidence is crucial. Otherwise, his colleagues will not take the concept seriously. He should be aware of what must be done and how it can be effective.

## Benefits of Effective Communication:

There are many facets of life, both personal and professional, in which effective communication is important. Improving communication skills has numerous benefits and can help individuals, groups, and organizations. The following are some of the most important benefits:

### Building Trust:

Clear communication fosters trust by ensuring transparency and understanding between individuals. Building trust between people begins with open and honest communication, which lays the groundwork for openness and understanding. Any relationship needs trust, which is a sensitive but necessary component that grows through clear and efficient communication. Communication clarity is equally important. You are more likely to be understood by others when you communicate clearly and concisely. When you communicate clearly, there is less chance of misinterpretation, and the other person will accurately grasp and convey what you have said. Since it sets expectations and establishes a shared sense of certainty, this shared understanding is essential for fostering trust.

Additionally, attentive listening is a key element of effective communication and is essential to developing trust. Your interpersonal relationship is strengthened when you feel understood and heard. Engaging in active listening to others' viewpoints will increase your empathy and demonstrate your sincere curiosity about their ideas and emotions, which will strengthen the bonds of trust between you and them. Conversely, being open and honest when giving information is a fundamental component of transparent communication. Also, transparent communication provides insight into your objectives, ideas, and behaviours, enhancing authenticity. Because it demonstrates a commitment to open communication and a willingness to be candid, this transparency builds credibility and fosters confidence.

### Conflict Resolution:

It facilitates conflict resolution by encouraging open dialogue and mutual understanding. Since it promotes candid discussion and mutual understanding among the parties involved, effective communication is essential to resolving conflicts. Clear presentation of your ideas and concerns is vital for conflict resolution, and good communication provides the means to express these feelings. A forum for the expression of individual viewpoints, needs, and complaints is established when you hold an open discussion. To communicate effectively, it is important for others to hear you speak and to understand your intentions and feelings as well. This is achieved through active listening. In addition to helping identify the fundamental problems fueling the disagreement, this also broadens your perspective.

Additionally, effective communication encourages empathy, which is crucial for comprehending and appreciating different people's perspectives, emotions, and ideas. Through cooperation, a shared goal of finding common ground replaces the previous adversarial conflict resolution approach. You can approach disagreements with a more positive and solution-focused perspective when you communicate, as it promotes non-defensive reactions. Moreover, effective communication reduces the possibility of misconceptions, which frequently result in conflicts, by helping to define and explain expectations. As an instrument for group problem-solving, it is useful. You can jointly brainstorm, weigh possibilities, and come to compromises that serve the interests of all parties involved by having honest and open discussions with the other person. Together with resolving your current issues, this cooperative strategy lays the groundwork for future exchanges based on mutual respect and understanding.

### Strengthening Relationships:

Empathetic communication nurtures deeper connections and promotes emotional support. It is a strong force that transcends simple talk, building deep connections and providing the vital emotional support needed in relationships. Empathetic communication entails building a bridge that goes beyond words alone by having the capacity to comprehend and experience another person's emotions. When you communicate with empathy, you show that you genuinely want to understand the feelings and experiences of people around you.

Active listening, in which you pay attention to the underlying emotions being expressed in addition to just hearing what is being said, is another characteristic of this type of communication. Empathetic communication conveys a strong feeling of acceptance and understanding in both you and the other person by recognizing and affirming these feelings. Because it shows that your sentiments are not only heard but also appreciated, this acknowledgement fosters a deeper connection between you and other people. Empathetic communication is essential for building strong relationships and providing emotional support. It establishes a secure environment where people can express their vulnerabilities without worrying about being judged. People feel seen and heard when they are shown empathy, and this affirmation enhances their mental health and sense of belonging. Empathetic communication is a calming presence during difficult times and an amplifier of celebrations during happy ones.

## Tips for Improving Interpersonal Relationships

### 1. Active Listening:

Try listing things efficiently. It necessitates that you be patient initially, maintain composure, and allow the other person to express all their emotions without interfering. Alternatively, active listening entails genuinely nodding and leaning forward to adopt an attentive listening attitude. These gestures will offer nonverbal indications that the speaker is being appropriately listened to. Practice active listening by giving your undivided attention, showing genuine interest, and refraining from interrupting. Validate others' feelings and perspectives.

### 2. Clarity and Conciseness:

Try communicating your thoughts and ideas clearly and concisely. To communicate effectively, one must be clear and concise.

These constitute the fundamental elements that guarantee your thoughts are understandable to your audience. You demonstrate your clarity when you communicate your ideas clearly and concisely, avoiding any possibility of doubt or misunderstanding. Avoid ambiguity and use language that is not easily understandable to the listener. To deliver your intended message without ambiguity, you must use precise word choice and manner of speaking. However, this requires you to communicate your views succinctly and directly, omitting any extraneous information that could overshadow your primary message. To make the message impactful and easy to understand, it encourages you to eliminate unnecessary details and use only what is necessary.

You can improve comprehension and engagement by emphasizing conciseness and clarity. Being succinct shows respect for your listener's time and attention, while being clear promotes productive collaboration and avoid misunderstandings. Your skill in communication lies in providing your audience with a shared understanding by succinctly and precisely expressing your ideas, whether you are conveying everyday information or complex concepts.

### 3. Empathy and Understanding:

Empathy fosters deeper connections and resolves conflicts more effectively. Harmonious relationships and successful dispute resolution are based on empathy and understanding. Put yourself in others' shoes to understand their emotions and viewpoints. The ability to understand another's perspectives and feelings is known as empathy. It facilitates the development of strong interpersonal relationships. Show sincere interest in the experiences and emotions of others by engaging in active listening and recognizing a range of opinions. Try to understand the viewpoint of another individual. It will cultivate empathy and break down communication barriers.

This kind of approach will improve your interpersonal connections and make conflict resolution go more smoothly. Feeling understood makes it easier for you and others to work together freely to identify win-win solutions, preventing disputes before they escalate. Empathy acts as a bridge in both the personal and professional spheres, encouraging a culture of deference and thoughtfulness toward others that will aid in your personal growth.

Your communication experience is also enhanced when you pay attention to nonverbal signs. You may be confident that messages are not only heard but also fully comprehended as a result of fostering a stronger relationship. The way your messages are received and comprehended is greatly influenced by nonverbal communication, which is a silent but powerful force. To add levels of meaning beyond spoken words, one must incorporate a range of cues, such as your posture, tone of voice, gestures, and facial expressions.

Your ability to communicate effectively depends on your ability to read these nonverbal cues. Examine others' motions and facial expressions. Pay attention to non-verbal cues—facial expressions, gestures, and body language. Your facial expressions, which convey happiness, surprise, melancholy, or irritation, act as a visual symphony of your feelings. A raised eyebrow, a scowl, or a glowered expression can convey a lot and provide important details about the speaker's inner condition.

Similarly, gestures enhance spoken words by emphasizing points, making things clearer, or even providing cultural context. While a sweeping hand gesture can firmly emphasize a point, a simple nod can confirm understanding. Thoughts and sentiments are also reflected in body language, a silent yet powerful communicator.

Align your non-verbal communication with your verbal messages to ensure consistency. These nonverbal clues must be in perfect harmony with spoken words for communication to be genuinely effective. Building trust and improving the clarity of the intended message are two benefits of consistency in verbal and nonverbal communication. Alternatively, misalignment might cause misunderstandings or confusion, which lessens the communication's overall impact.

### 4. Open and Honest Communication:

Encourage open and honest communication in relationships. Express thoughts and feelings authentically while being respectful of others' perspectives. Establish trust, fostering collaboration, and create a positive interpersonal environment, all of which depend on open and honest communication. You must employ a diverse approach to foster such transparency. Build a community where people feel safe enough to open up and trust one another. When you feel safe and assured that your ideas and opinions will be valued, you are more likely to express yourself honestly. By valuing other viewpoints, offering constructive criticism, and actively listening, leaders can set the tone.

As previously discussed, the foundation of transparent communication is active listening. Promote uninterrupted speech both for yourself and other people, and show that you genuinely care about what they have to say. Provide a direct and transparent line of contact. Whether it is through frequent team meetings, one-on-one conversations, or anonymous suggestion boxes, provide people with different spaces to express themselves. Various routes of communication allow for varying degrees of comfort and preference. Consider constructive criticism. It is an effective instrument for encouraging honesty. Establish a feedback culture where improvement is prioritized over criticism. Address areas for improvement while highlighting the good parts of performance. This strategy encourages people to ask for help without fear of retaliation and to discuss their experiences openly. It can also have transformative effects when a leader exhibits vulnerability. A culture of transparency is fostered when leaders discuss their struggles and lessons learned. In return, team members are more willing to share their own experiences, which promotes a friendly and open atmosphere.

### 5. Conflict Resolution Skills:

Try gaining experience in resolving your conflicts. Develop conflict resolution skills by practising active listening, finding common ground, and focusing on solutions rather than blame. A combination of self-awareness, skill at communicating, and dedication to constructive problem-solving are required in this dynamic and continuous process. Developing self-awareness should come first. Recognizing your personal biases, triggers, and communication style is crucial. Your ability to effectively manage conflicts will be built upon it. Try to understand other people's viewpoints without passing judgment right away. Be receptive to a greater awareness of the feelings and worries that others are experiencing. Be receptive to criticism and articulating ideas and emotions straightforwardly and forcefully. Aim for finding answers that both parties may agree on through cooperative problem-solving. Also, adopt a solution-focused mentality in which disagreements are seen as opportunities for your advancement rather than as roadblocks. This approach promotes an optimistic outlook. Make the most of opportunities to hone your abilities by participating in role-playing games or asking mentors and coworkers for feedback. Finally, adopt a mindset of perpetual learning. You have the option to keep improving your skills by reflecting on previous disagreements, examining effective solutions, and adjusting your tactics in response to criticism.

### 6. Feedback and Validation:

Provide constructive feedback and validation. Give positive reinforcement and constructive criticism, which may require striking a careful balance between praising efforts and making recommendations for development. Acknowledge others' efforts and communicate feedback in a way that is helpful and supportive. Start by identifying and stating clearly the good things about the work that has been done. Please elaborate on what impressed you. Emphasize both the procedure and the result. This will start things off well and lay the groundwork for helpful criticism. Try not to make your criticism personal while giving constructive feedback; instead, focus on the behaviour or result. Give precise details on the areas in which improvement is needed and support your arguments with concise examples. Instead of provoking defensiveness, constructive criticism should be phrased to support your development. Make use of language that is solution-focused, impartial, and nonjudgmental. Saying something like, "Meeting deadlines consistently is crucial," could be a better way to phrase it than, "You always miss deadlines."

It is equally important to acknowledge the effort and goal of the work. Let them know how much you value their diligence and commitment. You will create a more upbeat and encouraging environment because of this recognition, which will increase your openness to helpful criticism. You should also think about using the "feedback sandwich" strategy, which involves sandwiching constructive criticism between encouraging remarks. This will emphasize a collaborative approach to growth and help tobalance the perceived negative. Give an affirmation. Show empathy and respect by acknowledging the thoughts and feelings of others. Say something like, "I understand," or "I value your viewpoint," tovalidate their experiences.

Effective communication is the foundation of harmonious relationships. By embracing clear, empathetic communication practices and honing interpersonal skills, individuals can nurture stronger connections, resolve conflicts amicably, and foster a culture of trust and understanding in their relationships.

# Chapter 8:
# Financial Well-being

*"Financial freedom is available to those who learn about it and work for it." – Robert Kiyosaki*

There is a great deal of uncertainty about the future. However, you may prepare yourself as much as possible for it. Financial well-being plays a crucial role in our overall development, impacting various aspects of our lives beyond mere monetary transactions. Financial planning is a way to manage your money carefully and reach your life's objectives. It is a vital resource for all of us and a fantastic means of fortifying, forming, and safeguarding our future. "By failing to prepare, you are preparing to fail," as Benjamin Franklin famously said. *Planning your funds for a stable future is crucial as a result. It influences our choices, opportunities, and peace of mind, intertwining with our growth journey.*

Financial well-being comes with proper financial planning. It is an idea that offers direction and a plan of action for personal budgeting, insurance, retirement, savings, and other financial matters. Your finances include, in essence, all aspects of the economics of your lifestyle expenses, savings, and investments.

## Relationship between Financial Health and Personal Development:

### Freedom and Opportunities:

Good and stable financial health provides freedom to pursue goals, invest in personal growth, and explore opportunities. You can achieve personal empowerment and self-development through maintaining sound financial health. It will provide you the freedom to go after your objectives, make investments in your development, and investigate new prospects. You will be able to focus on your goals without having to worry about money problems if you have a strong financial foundation that gives you a sense of security and stability.

The assurance it gives you to pursue your objectives is one of the main advantages of financial stability. If your finances are properly planned, you can achieve your goals, whether they involve starting a business, purchasing a home, or going back to school. Being financially independent not only makes you feel accomplished but also opens you to a world of opportunities. When you are financially stable, investing in your personal development becomes feasible. This could entail learning new skills, attending workshops, or pursuing higher education. Your ability to invest wisely in yourself and advance your knowledge and skills for both professional and personal development will be made possible by your financial stability. This makes you more capable of navigating the challenges presented by the paths you have chosen.

However, having good financial stability will also enable you to take advantage of opportunities that might not have been possible otherwise. Having a strong financial foundation gives you the freedom to seize great opportunities, whether you are establishing a business, investing in creative ideas, or taking measured risks. This ability to manage your finances comfortably will encourage you to pursue success by acting as a catalyst for entrepreneurship.

**Reduced Stress:**

Financial stability alleviates stress, allowing individuals to focus on personal development without constant financial worries. A stable financial situation gives you the mental and emotional room to focus on your growth, which effectively counteracting the constant stress brought on by your financial instability. You experience a considerable reduction in stress when your fundamental financial demands are satisfied, and you feel secure about the future. This is because your ongoing concern about making ends meet also lessens. Your focus and energy can be directed toward your development and progress when ongoing financial concerns do not burden you. You may concentrate on developing your abilities, going to school, and creating meaningful experiences rather than worrying about money problems. Your general well-being and mental toughness will improve because of this change in perspective.

The establishment and accomplishment of personal development objectives will be facilitated by financial stability. Those who have a solid financial foundation are better prepared to take on transformative journeys, whether they involve learning new skills, pursuing passions, or making investments in their health and well-being. Financial stability may prove to be one of the greatest sources of inspiration for your empowerment, giving you the confidence and purpose to face life's obstacles head-on.

### Long-Term Planning:

Financial well-being can form the bedrock for your strategic long-term planning. It will provide you with the essential tools to navigate your future with confidence. It enables strategic long-term planning, fostering a sense of security and stability conducive to personal growth. When your financial health is robust, there is a heightened sense of security and stability that can create a conducive environment for your deliberate and forward-thinking decision-making.

Your financial stability also allows you to engage in comprehensive, strategic planning for the long term. This involves setting achievable goals, whether it be saving for retirement, investing in a home, or creating an education fund. Such planning is underpinned by the confidence that comes with knowing there are resources to support these aspirations, reducing the uncertainties that often impede long-term strategizing. On the other hand, financial well-being also fosters a mindset of stability, enabling you to weather economic fluctuations and unforeseen challenges. This resilience can contribute to a sense of security, freeing you from the constant stress of financial instability and creating mental space for personal growth initiatives.

Your ability to plan for the long term not only provides a sense of direction but also facilitates intentional investments in personal development. Individuals can allocate resources for educational pursuits, skill development, and experiences that contribute to their overall growth. This deliberate approach to personal development is buoyed by the financial security that underlies your strategic long-term planning, creating a virtuous cycle of stability and growth in your life. Ultimately, financial well-being serves as a linchpin for a future-oriented, personally fulfilling journey.

## Guidance on Budgeting, Saving, and Investing Wisely

These are some of the strategies that can help you for your betterment:

### 1. Budgeting:

Create a comprehensive budget outlining income, expenses, and savings goals. Prioritize needs over wants, allocate funds accordingly, and track spending to stay within budgetary limits. Note down all of your sources of income, including your salary and any additional money you make, to establish a thorough budget. List your fixed costs, including your rent, utilities, and loan payments. Sort variable costs into requirements (groceries, utilities) and wants (entertainment, eating out). Make sure your needs are met before you commit money to wants by giving necessities top priority when allocating expenditures. A certain percentage of your income should be set away for savings, including long-term objectives and emergency cash. Utilize applications or budgeting tools to keep a regular check on your expenditures and adhere to set spending limitations. Prioritize debt repayment and make necessary adjustments to the budget as circumstances change. Building up an emergency reserve is a great way to prevent using credit for unanticipated costs. Consulting a professional can offer tailored advice on how to maximize your budget and reach your financial objectives. An effective balance between income, expenses, and savings is achieved with the aid of this methodical technique, which also encourages financial discipline.

## 2. Emergency Fund and Savings:

Create a rainy-day fund to deal with unexpected costs. Put some money aside monthly and set up automatic savings to create a safety net. Establish a routine of putting aside a specific amount of your income on a monthly basis to create an emergency fund and safeguard yourself from unforeseen expenses. Based on your needs and financial circumstances, start by setting a reasonable monthly savings target. To make this process more efficient, the movement of funds from your checking to a savings account can be set up to happen automatically. You may ensure that creating a financial buffer is done consistently and systematically by automating savings. Choose an easily accessible savings account that is distinct from your primary checking account. Gather three to six months' worth of living expenses to cover unexpected costs like medical bills, car repairs, or losing your job. By acting as a safety net, this fund helps people avoid having to rely on loans or credit cards in trying times. To strengthen your financial security and resilience, review and modify your savings goals regularly as your financial situation changes.

### 3. Debt Management:

Manage and minimize debt by making timely payments, and avoiding unnecessary borrowing. People can recover control over their finances and strive toward becoming debt-free by taking a proactive and disciplined approach to managing their debt, which includes making regular payments and refraining from taking on excessive borrowing. A planned approach centered on prioritizing, making timely payments, and using prudent borrowing practices is necessary for effectively managing and lowering your debt. Prioritize paying off high-interest obligations first, such as credit card debt, by first recognizing them. Loans must be paid off as soon as possible because they can mount up quickly. Create a budget that allows a sizeable percentage of your income to pay off debt. To prevent late fines and additional interest costs, timely payments are essential. Make sure you never forget deadlines by setting up automatic payments or reminders. By differentiating between essential and non-essential spending, try to avoid borrowing money that is not needed. Make needs a higher priority than wants and avoid taking on more debt to pay for extravagant items. Reduce your dependency on credit for unforeseen financial difficulties by building an emergency fund to meet unforeseen costs.

### 4. Retirement Planning:

Start early with retirement planning. Contribute to retirement accounts or pension plans to secure future financial stability. Starting your retirement planning early is a critical first step in ensuring your financial security in the future. Start by learning about and investigating the retirement savings choices that are accessible to you.

## 5. Financial Education and Learning:

Continuously educate yourself about personal finance. Read books, attend workshops, or seek advice from financial advisors to make informed decisions. Maintaining your financial literacy is crucial to reaching financial well-being and making wise decisions regarding your finances. Make it a practice to read books about personal finance, including those that address investing, retirement planning, and budgeting. You can get useful methods and insights from books authored by credible financial writers.

Participate in webinars, seminars, or workshops led by organizations and financial professionals. These gatherings provide interactive education opportunities that let you learn about many facets of personal finance in a practical way and ask questions. Consult with financial consultants for guidance since their suggestions will be specific to your individual needs financial objectives, and circumstances. Use credible financial websites, blogs, and news sources to stay up to date on the latest news and trends in the financial industry. Get frequent updates and insights by subscribing to financial newsletters.

Participate in online networks and forums where people exchange advice and financial experiences. Engage in conversations to extend your horizons and get insight from the achievements and difficulties of others. You can establish a continuous learning loop that enables you to make wise and calculated decisions for your financial journey by combining these strategies, such asreading books, attending workshops, consulting financial advisors, keeping up with financial news, and participating in online communities.

## 6. Mindful Spending and Value Assessment:

Practice mindful spending by assessing the value of purchases. Prioritize spending on items or experiences aligned with long-term goals and values. Spending mindfully entails carefully weighing the benefits of purchases to make sure they support your values and long-term objectives. Start by outlining your values precisely and setting definite long-term objectives. Make a budget that allows money for your discretionary spending while giving priority to necessities. Keep a close eye on your spending to spot trends and areas where you may adjust. Consider whether a potential purchase is in line with your goals and values. Spending should be prioritized on things or activities that support your goals, well-being, or personal development. Apply the 24-hour rule to give yourself enough time to think things through before making unnecessary purchases. Prioritize experiences over material goods because they typically bring long-lasting fulfilment. Make sure your spending habits and budget are in line with your changing values and goals by reviewing them regularly. By cultivating an appreciation for what you currently have, you can reduce the desire for pointless purchases and promote contentment and wise financial decisions. Through the integration of these activities, you develop an intentional spending mindset that improves your financial well-being generally and is in line with your larger life goals.

Financial well-being is intricately linked to personal development. By implementing prudent financial practices such as budgeting, saving, debt management, and smart investing, individuals can pave the way for not only financial stability but also a conducive environment for personal growth, empowerment, and future success.

# Chapter 9:
# **Nurturing Relationships**

*"There is no exercise better for the heart than reaching down and lifting people up."*
*-John Andres Holmes*

Our relationships with other people provide us with a great deal of enjoyment and fulfillment. You can discover entirely new hobbies or develop ones you already have when you have strong emotional connections with people. They can even assist you in achieving success in your career or support you during your lowest moments.

You learn about other people's perspectives, passions, desires, and fears through the relationships you have with them. By delving into the thoughts and emotions of others, you frequently come out of the experience richer and more empathetic. To prevent hurting the people we care about, you grow gentler. You travel and experience new things.

Likewise, you learn about yourself, how you differ, and how you are similar to others by forming relationships with them. Additionally, you get more confident just by having other people recognize your worth. *The qualities our supervisors find admirable in our work help us to feel more confident in our own talents, just as our friends help us to realize the qualities, we are good at.* Relationships serve as the fabric of our lives. They weave connections that enrich our experiences and contribute significantly to our sense of fulfillment and well-being. They encompass connections with family, friends, colleagues, and broader communities.

## Impact of Relationships on Personal Fulfilment:

### Emotional Support and Understanding:

Healthy relationships offer emotional support, understanding, and a sense of belonging, nurturing your emotional well-being. Strong bonds with others provide you with vital components like empathy, understanding, and a deep sense of community, all of which are essential for maintaining your mental health. Your capacity to disclose your thoughts, feelings, and vulnerabilities in these connections without worrying about being judged is what makes them safe. The foundation of strong relationships is emotional support. It entails sharing triumphs, lending a sympathetic ear when necessary, and supporting one another during trying times. With your help, those who are associated with you will have a stronger base of trust and emotional resilience. Our capacity for understanding is encouraged.

An additional crucial element in a healthy relationship that supports your emotional well-being is understanding. In addition to identifying and accepting the other person's feelings, it entails trying to understand their viewpoints, experiences, and beliefs. Individuals' emotional bonds will be strengthened by this mutual understanding, which promotes empathy. You can feel heard and accepted in your healthy relationships by exchanging experiences and having honest conversations that validate each other.

Having a sense of belonging is another benefit of having healthy relationships; they satisfy a basic human desire for social connection by having a profound, meaningful connection to others. This sense of belonging will boost your self-image and increase your confidence to face life's obstacles. Your emotional well-being is reinforced by the community that you will discover in good relationships, which promotes personal development and growth.

**Growth and Learning:**

Interactions with others will provide opportunities for your growth, learning, and expanding perspectives through diverse experiences and viewpoints. Whether through brief meetings or long-term partnerships, human contacts provide a rich tapestry of varied experiences and perspectives that greatly aid in your personal growth.

Social interactions can be quite beneficial for your personal development, self-improvement, ongoing education, and broadening of your viewpoints.

Being exposed to different viewpoints is one of the main ways that interactions promote progress. Every individual contributes their own set of values, experiences, and beliefs. Interacting with people from other countries, backgrounds, and walks of life exposes one to a wealth of fresh perspectives and ideas. Diversity broadens your cognitive horizons and challenges your preconceptions, which encourages a never-ending process of learning and adaptation.

It also provides you a platform to share your knowledge and abilities with others. You can gain knowledge from other people through group projects, mentoring, or informal discussions. Your ability to learn new abilities and hone your current ones can both result from these exchanges. In today's environment of rapid change, this will also aid in development a flexible and adaptable attitude. Furthermore, the difficulties and disagreements that can occur in social situations contribute to personal development.

**Fulfillment and Happiness:**

Strong relationships often correlate with your higher levels of happiness and life satisfaction, contributing to your overall personal fulfillment. It is impossible to exaggerate the importance of healthy relationships in promoting pleasure and life satisfaction. To be happy and satisfied with life, you need strong relationships. They are essential to your entire sense of fulfillment. There is a strong correlation between the quality of your relationships and your overall sense of well-being. These relationships provide companionship, emotional support, and shared experiences that serve as pillars in your quest for happiness. Your strong relationships and higher levels of happiness are correlated due to your basic human urge for belonging.

They build a network of support for you during both happy and difficult moments. These interactions offer with emotional support that helps you become more resilient, which lessens the impact of life's unavoidable setbacks and improves your ability to handle stress.

Moreover, common experiences in solid relationships also elevate your feelings of happiness and contentment. Whether it is sharing laughs, overcoming challenges as a team, or celebrating successes, these group encounters create a bank of good memories that enhance your sense of fulfillment in life. Deep connection and companionship are fostered in romantic relationships through intimacy, mutual understanding, and trust. Additionally, friendships provide a unique camaraderie where mutual respect and common interests foster a happy social life.

Strong relationships have been associated with improved physical health as well as emotional well-being, highlighting their comprehensive influence on well-being. These relationships offer social and emotional support that can improve immune system performance, reduce the risk of mental health problems, and contribute to a longer, healthier life.

## Insights on Fostering Healthy Connections

A blueprint for building deep connections that enhance general well-being is provided by insights on creating healthy connections, which are essential for navigating the complicated terrain of interpersonal interactions. Comprehending the fundamentals of productive communication, empathy, and reciprocal regard facilitates the establishment and maintenance of enduring relationships. Here are a few strategies for fostering positive relationships:

## 1. Communication and Empathy:

Practice open, honest communication and empathy in relationships. Listen actively, express emotions honestly, and seek to understand perspectives. You cannot have healthy relationships, understanding, and connection with other people without open, honest communication and empathy. Adhere to these guidelines to foster an atmosphere where viewpoints are respected, and you and others openly express emotions. Engaging fully with the speaker is a crucial aspect of active listening. Show that you care about other people's opinions and feelings by giving them your full attention. By doing this, you demonstrate that you are committed to appreciating and comprehending other people's experiences.

Being truthful in your expression of emotion promotes an environment of sincerity and trust. Be open about your sentiments; a deeper relationship will be possible as a result. Building the foundation for deep conversations involves having the courage to express one's pleasures, vulnerabilities, and concerns. You can build connections and mutual support by being open and honest about your emotions with others.

Additionally, empathy has transformative power in relationships. It involves not only being aware of other people's feelings but also putting yourself in their shoes to understand what they are thinking. Make an effort to communicate with empathy; it will transcend simple pity. It requires an honest attempt to comprehend and give credence to the thoughts, feelings, and experiences of another individual. Share what you understand with others and try to comprehend different points of view. Actively participate in discussions that delve into various perspectives to embrace diversity and contribute to the rich tapestry of shared experiences. By embracing diversity, this inclusive attitude will expand your horizons and encourage personal development while promoting harmony.

## 2. Mutual Respect and Boundaries:

Respect others' opinions, boundaries, and individuality. Establish clear boundaries while respecting the boundaries set by others. Respect the beliefs, limits, and uniqueness of others. Building wholesome connections requires it. Develop an attitude that respects differences in opinion to start. Seek to understand rather than persuade others by actively listening to opposing viewpoints without passing judgment. Recognize that the varied experiences and viewpoints of individuals shape their opinions.

Set your own distinct boundaries and express them in an honest, firm manner when it comes to boundaries. Recognize and honor others' boundaries at the same time. Respect people's demand for privacy or personal space and refrain from pushing them to step beyond their comfort zones. It is important to communicate consistently, ask them about their boundaries, and be open to any changes they might need.

Respecting each person's distinctiveness will help you to embrace and cherish individuality. Accept that everyone has unique values, tastes, and life trajectories. Refrain from assuming anything about people and give them room to be themselves. You help create a peaceful, welcoming workplace where everyone feels appreciated and understood by maintaining respect for beliefs, boundaries, and individuality.

## 3. Quality Time and Presence:

Prioritize quality time spent with loved ones. Be present and engaged during interactions to foster deeper connections. Make time for your loved ones a top priority. Take intentional steps to develop stronger relationships with them. Start by setting up specific times on your calendar. Treat them as unchangeable obligations.

Reduce the number of distractions, such as electronic gadgets, and ensure your entire attention is on the current engagement during these times. Listen intently, keep your eyes open, and show that you genuinely care about their opinions and experiences. Engage in various activities with them to foster enduring memories and a sense of community. Shared activities can improve the quality of time spent with one another.

Another important factor is mindfulness. Live in the moment while being conscious. Enjoy the shared experience, without interruptions. To strengthen emotional ties, show affection both verbally and physically. Finally, consider creating customs or rituals to instill a feeling of expectation and constancy. By implementing these deliberate habits, you create an atmosphere that strengthens and nurtures the relationships you have with your loved ones, in addition to prioritizing quality time.

### 4. Support and Encouragement:

Offer support, encouragement, and validation to those in your circle. Celebrate their successes and assist during challenging times. Give others in your orbit your encouragement, support, and affirmation. Building healthy relationships is based on this. Offer them heartfelt celebration and show sincere gratitude for all that they have accomplished. Reassure them that their achievements are appreciated and acknowledged by sharing in their happiness. Offer unwavering support and a sympathetic ear when things are difficult. Just be there without passing judgment, and show compassion and understanding. Reassure them that their difficulties are understood and shared by validating their emotions and experiences. Assist them practically when necessary to show that you care about their welfare. Constant support also helps people feel resilient and empowered. Give them words of encouragement that highlight their qualities and strengths. Reiterate your belief in their capacity to overcome obstacles and encourage them to continue in the face of hardship. In the end, you aid in their and your own personal growth by fostering a nurturing atmosphere that honors accomplishments and offers consolation during trying times.

### 5. Conflict Resolution and Forgiveness:

Develop conflict resolution skills and practice forgiveness. Address conflicts calmly, find common ground, and be willing to forgive and move forward. Practice forgiving others and learning how to resolve conflicts. It is necessary to keep relationships in good shape. Deal with disagreements in a composed and confident manner first. By remaining calm and communicating your opinions or concerns in a non-confrontational way, you can prevent tensions from rising. It is essential to listen actively. Make an effort to comprehend what the other person is saying and remain receptive to helpful discussion. Find a point of agreement to overcome disputes. Find common ground or interests that might act as a basis for cooperation and compromise. Stress the significance of resolving conflicts amicably rather than concentrating just on personal preferences.

A useful tactic in resolving disputes is forgiveness. Develop an openness to pardon and let go of grudges. Recognize that forgiving someone releases you from the emotional burden of harboring resentment, not from endorsing the behavior. Openly express your forgiveness to others, creating a healing and understanding environment. When resolving conflicts, communicate effectively. To foster a non-defensive and blame-free atmosphere, use "I" statements to communicate your wants and feelings. As you collaborate to discover solutions that honor the requirements of both sides, encourage the other person to express their viewpoint. Lastly, set clear boundaries and expectations to prevent future disagreements. Create a culture of open communication in your relationships so that issues can be resolved more easily when they arise. You may increase the resilience and strength of your relationships and foster an atmosphere that is supportive of understanding and growth by learning conflict resolution techniques and accepting forgiveness.

### 6: Cultivate Trust and Reliability:

You may earn people's trust by always doing what you say you are going to do. Keep commitments and be someone others can rely on. Establishing strong, meaningful connections requires establishing trust established through consistency and dependability. Maintaining promises is one important factor. Make sure you always follow through on commitments and promises you make. This consistency creates a history of dependability that others may rely on, strengthening their faith in your moral character. It is as important that you interact consistently. Show that you are a reliable and trustworthy person in the lives of others around you. Reliability extends beyond significant commitments to include regular interactions and duties. Maintaining consistency conveys predictability to others, letting them know they can rely on you in a variety of circumstances.

Talk about your strengths and weaknesses honestly and openly. Regarding your commitments, be reasonable, open, and honest in your communication in the event of unforeseen events. Being upfront in communication and exhibiting accountability are two ways that openness fosters trust. Being someone that people can regularly rely on is, at its core, the key to developing trust. You may build a trustworthy environment that gradually improves your relationships by acting in accordance with your statements, honoring agreements, and being a consistent presence.

### 7. Gratitude and Appreciation:

Show your appreciation and thankfulness to those who are important to you. Recognize their contributions and show genuine appreciation. One of the most effective ways to build relationships and create a pleasant atmosphere is to show your gratitude and appreciation for the people in your life. Start by truly appreciating and honoring their contributions. When expressing your gratitude, be specific and point out the particular deeds or attributes that you value. This specificity gives it a more intimate feel and demonstrates how sincere and thoughtful your thanks are. Express your gratitude to people around you regularly to let them know that their efforts are valued. Saying "thank you" aloud for a favor or expressing your sincere appreciation for their influence on your life emphasizes the importance you place on their existence.

Consider making thoughtful gestures to show your gratitude. This could be organizing a unique outing, writing a heartfelt note, or giving a small gift. Make these gestures tailored to the recipient, showing that you have taken the time and care to convey your thanks. Adopt a positive and thankful mindset to incorporate gratitude into your everyday interactions. Remind yourself of the positive aspects of your relationships and express your thanks regularly. By cultivating the culture of appreciation, you can create a positive, supportive environment where people feel valued and acknowledged for their contributions to your life

Remember that nurturing healthy relationships is essential for your fulfillment. By fostering connections based on communication, empathy, mutual respect, and support, individuals can create a nurturing environment that enhances their well-being, growth, and overall satisfaction in life.

# Chapter 10:
# Continuous Learning

*The world is a university and everyone in it is a teacher. Make sure when you wake up in the morning you go to school. ~Bishop T.D. Jakes*

One thing I have discovered is that, in my quest to improve my life, I am learning new things that are crucial to that improvement on a regular basis. It is significantly enhancing my potential. Self-learning is a blend of self-teaching and self-trying, according to Connor Edsall, a biologist and geneticist, in his TED Talk. To bolster his argument, Edsall also cites the experiences of four people who altered the course of history despite having little or no formal education.

According to him, these four individuals used self-learning to attain remarkable success in their respective industries. Michael Faraday came first; he laid the groundwork for the physics idea of the electromagnetic field. Through experimental observation, Faraday built his hypotheses.

Next, he discussed John Hunter. He gained notoriety as the founder of scientific surgery. Hunter used experimentation, dissection, and observation to achieve this.

The Wright brothers, who created, constructed, and piloted the first successful aeroplane in history, are the others. Their parents had always encouraged them to design and build, and they would frequently work together on small projects like making paper folding machines, manufacturing kites, and replicating rubber band helicopters as toys.

"We have access to a vast amount of information nowadays," Edsall continues. "But learning is not only about ingesting knowledge. It would help if you put what you have learned into practice to truly learn. That is, you must conduct experiments and observe. You must attempt."

## The Value of Lifelong Learning

Your ability to adapt, develop, and prosper in a world that is constantly changing depends on your ability to learn throughout your life. It includes an attitude that prioritizes learning outside of the classroom, personal development, and curiosity. Continual personal and professional improvement throughout your life is the essence of lifelong learning, a vital pursuit that extends beyond your formal education. Continuously expanding one's knowledge offers many advantages, going beyond merely acquiring degrees or certifications.

First, continuing your education ensures that you will be flexible and well-prepared to handle the challenges of a rapidly changing world, especially in the information and technology domain. You should strive to become an insatiable learner. Lifelong learners welcome new abilities, tools, and approaches while also cultivating intellectually stimulating curiosity. Additionally, pursuing lifelong learning can significantly impact your happiness and well-being. Seeking information enhances one's sense of accomplishment and self-worth, irrespective of the method— whether formal classes, self-directed learning, or experiential learning. It can lead to a richer and more meaningful life and serves as a continuous source of intellectual stimulation for you.

The improvement of your career opportunities and job satisfaction in this professional setting is a clear indication of the significance of lifelong learning. You can increase your marketability and adaptability in a competitive job market by maintaining up-to-date industry trends and continuously developing your skills. Employers are placing a greater emphasis on workers who have a dedication to learning since it shows that they can innovate and make valuable contributions to the expansion of the company. In a world where industries are changing quickly, flexibility is a critical quality that may be fostered in you. It will help you become resilient and enhance your capacity to flourish in a variety of settings by motivating you to welcome change rather than run away from it.

Additionally, lifelong learning fosters a tolerant and open-minded community. One's worldview is expanded through exposure to many viewpoints and ideas, which promotes empathy and understanding. In a diverse and interconnected global society, this fosters social cohesiveness in addition to personal development.

## Importance of Lifelong Learning:

In the modern world, lifelong learning is crucial for these few strong reasons:

### Adaptation to Change:

Continuous learning fosters adaptability, allowing individuals to navigate changing circumstances and embrace new opportunities. Your ability to adjust to changing circumstances and take advantage of new chances in a world that is constantly changing is based on your continuous learning. The capacity to learn and apply new information is critical in a dynamic world where market trends, societal upheavals, and technology breakthroughs occur often. Continuing your studies beyond graduation guarantees that you will be adaptable and able to face new challenges. It gives you the tools necessary to adjust to changing market conditions, industry standards, and employment requirements. Adopting a mindset that prioritizes lifelong learning will help you succeed in your future undertakings, in addition to remaining relevant in your current responsibilities.

Moreover, creativity and problem-solving abilities are highly related to your adaptability. Change is more likely to be welcomed by continuous learners, who see difficulties as chances for improvement rather than as barriers. Their ability to adapt tactics, integrate new technologies, and explore fresh ideas allows them to promote innovation across a range of fields. Additionally, lifelong learning broadens your viewpoint and opens new perspectives for you. You can develop a comprehensive awareness of the world by being exposed to a variety of concepts, cultures, and disciplines. By encouraging open-mindedness and the capacity to recognize alternative points of view, this more inclusive perspective can help you become more adaptable.

**Personal Growth and Fulfillment:**

Continuous learning fuels personal growth, expands horizons, and contributes to a sense of fulfillment and purpose. It is the force behind your personal development, widening your horizons and giving your life a deep feeling of meaning and purpose. You may fully realize your potential by actively participating in continuous education, which will set you on a path of self-improvement and self-discovery.

This ongoing quest for information leads to an expanded skill set and improved adaptability by encouraging the development of new skills in addition to refining already acquired ones. Learning will help you see the world from a wider angle, fostering an open mind and a profound respect for other people's cultures and points of view. Continuous learning is a purposeful path that enhances your sense of purpose and fulfillment. Continuous learning can be accomplished through experiential learning, self-directed study, or formal education. It is a life-changing activity that can enable you to set and fulfill important goals. It will provide the energy for an endless cycle of personal development, bringing your growth and purpose together to create a life that is meaningful, dynamic, and ever-changing.

**Skill Enhancement and Innovation:**

Lifelong learning equips individuals with new skills and knowledge, fostering innovation and professional development. By offering a platform for the acquisition of new skills and information throughout your career, lifelong learning can catalyze your continual innovation and professional growth, motivating you in the process. *Settling down is not an option in a world that is changing so quickly; lifelong learning is a vital tool for adapting.* By introducing you to cutting-edge concepts, tools, and processes, continuing education fosters an innovative culture. It promotes taking the initiative to solve problems and being open to trying out new approaches. Lifelong learners are better suited to identify areas that could use improvement, which could propel you forward in your careers.

Moreover, professional progress is directly linked to the acquisition of new skills via lifetime learning. If you embrace lifelong learning, you will stay adaptable and resilient as industries and employment needs change. This dedication to study improves both your technical proficiency and soft skills, whether through workshops, online courses, or practical experiences.

By broadening your knowledge base and increasing your adaptability to shifting employment markets, lifelong learning also helps you advance in your career. It cultivates a growth mindset by ingraining the idea that skills may be acquired through effort and commitment. Employers highly value professionals who demonstrate a dedication to lifelong learning. They acknowledge the possibility of innovation and ongoing progress. The dynamic power of your lifetime learning fuels your continuous professional growth and creativity. You may both stay relevant in your occupations and advance your industries by actively seeking out new knowledge and abilities.

## Resources and Strategies for Ongoing Personal Development

### 1. Reading and Self-Education:

Read widely and diversely. Explore books, articles, blogs, and online resources covering various topics of interest. Platforms like TED Talks, Coursera, or Khan Academy offer a plethora of educational content. Adopt a diversified and broad reading strategy and take a multimodal approach to learning. Investigate a variety of subjects related to your interests and curiosities by reading books, articles, blogs, and internet resources. Books on various topics are abundant in physical and digital libraries, giving you access to a diversity of viewpoints and cultural backgrounds. For up-to-date information on current events and new trends, subscribe to reputable periodicals and publications.

You can meet people who have different perspectives and recommendations by participating in forums, reading clubs, or discussion groups. To cultivate a more comprehensive understanding of the world, push yourself to investigate subjects outside of your comfort zone. You can develop the habit of reading broadly and diversely by implementing these tactics, which will help you broaden and continuously increase your knowledge.

### 2. Networking and Communities:

Engage in communities, forums, or local groups related to your interests or industry. Networking exposes you to different perspectives and learning opportunities. These are effective tactics to help you advance both personally and professionally. Participate in lively discussion in social media groups, internet forums, or local meetups that support your work or passions. By networking in these communities, you can gain access to a variety of viewpoints, experiences, and educational opportunities.

Participate in debates, impart your knowledge, and ask community members for help. The sharing of ideas creates a setting where people can learn from each other and build on each other's strengths. You can also stay up-to-date on industry trends, new technology, and best practices by taking part in these communities. Through networking in these groups, one can find important relationships, possible partnerships, and mentorships. It opens doors to new opportunities, including joint ventures, business collaborations, and employment chances. Developing connections with like-minded people broadens your professional network and provides tools and opportunities for further education. You can foster a culture of continuous learning and cooperation by actively participating in groups that are relevant to your hobbies or line of work. By taking a proactive approach to networking, you may build stronger professional relationships and expand your knowledge base, which will help you on a dynamic and comprehensive path of personal and professional development.

### 3. Mentorship and Coaching:

Seek mentorship or coaching from experienced individuals. Mentors offer guidance, share insights, and provide invaluable support for personal and professional growth. Getting coaching or mentoring from professionals is a wise step toward both career and personal development. Find possible mentors whose areas of expertise align with your objectives, and then politely approach them. Give a clear explanation of your goals and the areas in which you need help.

Show your excitement and openness to learning while emphasizing the benefits of the mentorship for both parties. Plan a regular communication schedule and be ready to participate fully in the educational process. Accept constructive criticism as an opportunity for growth and maintain an open mind when receiving it. Take advantage of the mentor's experiences, engage in intelligent conversations, and ask questions to learn more. By initiating a mentorship relationship, you can gain access to a wealth of information, insights, and useful guidance. Your learning curve may be accelerated, aiding you in overcoming obstacles and making wise decisions. To establish a solid and mutually beneficial partnership, show your appreciation for the mentor's time and efforts.

By proactively pursuing mentorship, you can benefit from the knowledge and experiences of those who have taken a similar path. In addition to accelerating your professional and personal development, the mentor-mentee dynamic fosters a strong support system that encourages ongoing learning and development.

### 4. Skill Development and Practice:

Learn something new or hone an old talent by practicing it often. Dedicate time regularly to practice and improve skills that align with your goals. Your practice must be deliberate and continuous, with the purpose of acquiring or honing existing abilities. Make time for goals-related activities on a regular and concentrated basis. Schedule dedicated time in your calendar to practice intentionally, focusing on the details of the talent you wish to get better at. Divide the ability into manageable parts, then methodically practice each one. Make use of tools that offer direction and helpful criticism, whether they come from mentorship, online courses, or practical experience. Adopt a growth mindset, understanding that progress requires perseverance and learning from mistakes. Track your development and pinpoint areas that need improvement by utilizing feedback loops. Celebrate your accomplishments, evaluate your performance on a regular basis, and modify your strategy considering new information. Over time, mastery is developed through consistent practice. Moreover, use a range of teaching strategies, including reading, applying in real life, and seeking mentoring. Join forums or groups where you can exchange experiences and gain knowledge from people who share your interests.

You can cultivate an attitude of continuous improvement and develop and improve your talents through consistent, deliberate practice. This systematic approach supports both professional and personal development, giving you the know-how to succeed in your chosen fields.

### 5. Podcasts and Audiobooks:

Listen to podcasts or audiobooks during commutes or downtime. They offer accessible and engaging ways to absorb new information and perspectives. These methods for passing the time during commutes or downtime are enjoyable and practical ways to learn new things. These audio formats offer easily accessible learning opportunities that fit into your everyday schedule, whether you are exercising, driving, or waiting. Podcasts span a wide range of subjects, including storytelling, self-improvement, science, and history. They frequently feature professionals, business titans, or hobbyists who talk candidly and eloquently about their experiences and thoughts. On the other hand, audiobooks can provide you with in-depth analyses of a variety of topics, often narrated by accomplished individuals who truly bring the material to life.

Because podcasts and audiobooks are auditory, you can multitask and make use of your downtime. This type of passive learning can be very helpful for acquiring new views, broadening your knowledge base, and staying up-to-date on current trends. Because you can tailor your learning experience and select content that fits your interests, it is an adaptable and inclusive learning technique. All in all, adding them to your everyday schedule turns downtime into opportunities for ongoing learning and mental challenges.

### 6. Reflection and Application:

Reflect on what you have learned and apply it to real-life situations. Application solidifies learning and reinforces its practicality. One of the most important learning processes is reflection, which turns theoretical information into practical abilities by applying what has been taught to real-world scenarios. Determine the main ideas, lessons learned, and insights from your experiences by carefully going over and summarizing them. Keeping a notebook or taking notes can assist with this introspective process. Next, think about how you may apply this newfound knowledge or abilities to your everyday activities or professional life. Determine pertinent situations or difficulties where the knowledge gained can be utilized. This step entails relating the theoretical knowledge to the pragmatic details of actual circumstances.

Moreover, seek out chances to put your knowledge into practice. Apply the ideas or abilities you have learned intentionally, whether it is for a job project, personal objective, or situation involving problem-solving. Accept the learning curve and be receptive to modifying your strategy, considering experience and feedback.

Evaluate your apps' results and efficacy on a regular basis. Consider your successes and areas for development. To create a constant feedback loop between theory and practice, modify your approach accordingly. Discuss your experiences and gain new insights by having conversations with peers, mentors, or online groups. This strengthens your comprehension while introducing you to a variety of applications and potential deviations in practical situations. You can improve the relevance and applicability of knowledge by actively putting what you have learned into practice. This approach makes learning a dynamic and ever-evolving experience, ensuring that the knowledge you acquire is integrated into your skill set and decision-making in everyday life. After all, the measure of mastery and lifelong learning is the ability to apply knowledge in various circumstances.

Lifelong learning is a commitment to growth and self-improvement throughout one's life. By leveraging a variety of resources and strategies—from books and courses to networking and reflection—individuals can embark on a continuous journey of personal development, fostering adaptability, innovation, and fulfillment throughout their lives.

# Conclusion:

Embarking on your self-development journey is a transformative commitment that begins with self-awareness, the cornerstone and initial step towards personal growth. Understanding who you are entirely sets the stage for meaningful goal setting, which brings you closer to your dreams. As you navigate through challenges, remember that obstacles can be opportunities in disguise, and failures can serve as valuable teaching moments.

Developing positive habits, cultivating emotional intelligence and mindfulness, and practicing gratitude are essential components that promote mental clarity, empathy, and a happier life. Effective communication fosters strong relationships and allows for precise, sympathetic interactions with others. Furthermore, maintaining financial stability and nurturing meaningful relationships contribute significantly to human growth and well-being.

Continuous learning is key to adaptability and progress. Learning from your experiences and embracing a lifetime of learning ensures that you evolve and grow. Your self-development journey is unique, filled with lessons, milestones, and opportunities for growth. Embrace each step with curiosity and resilience, celebrating each achievement along the way.

Personal development is a lifelong journey that requires dedication, adaptability, and a commitment to unlocking your true potential. Embrace each lesson, celebrate each milestone, and remain dedicated to continuous learning and self-improvement. Remember, your journey is unique—learn, adapt, and evolve to become the best version of yourself.